Belief in Psychology

Belief in Psychology

A Study in the Ontology of Mind

Jay L. Garfield

A Bradford Book
The MIT Press
Cambridge, Massachusetts
London, England

This book was set in Palatino by Asco Trade Typesetting Ltd. in Hong Kong and printed and bound by Halliday Lithograph in the United States of America.

Library of Congress Cataloging-in-Publication Data

Garfield, Jay L., 1955–
  Belief in psychology.

  "A Bradford Book."
  Bibliography: p.
  Includes index.
  1. Psychology—Philosophy. I. Title.
BF38.G295   1988   153′.01   87-26162
ISBN 0-262-07108-8

For Blaine

Contents

Preface

In the course of developing these ideas and this text I have incurred many significant intellectual and personal debts. An earlier version of this book served as my doctoral dissertation at the University of Pittsburgh. In the course of that project I received invaluable criticism and assistance from Nuel D. Belnap, Jr., and from John Haugeland, for which I am very grateful. Portions of this text appear in somewhat modified form in Stillings et al. 1987. I am grateful to The MIT Press for permission to reuse that material here.

Much of this research was completed while I was on sabbatical leave from Hampshire College, and was supported by grants from the college and from the Charles H. Dana Foundation. I am particularly grateful to President Adele Simmons, to Deans Penina Glazer, Harmon Dunathan, Mark Feinstein, and Richard Muller, and to Neil Stillings for their respective roles in supporting this research. Thanks also to the Academy of Finland, which provided additional research time to allow me to complete this work and to profit from valuable conversations with my Finnish colleagues concerning the manuscript, and to Timo Airaksinen for arranging my visit to Helsinki.

For significant logistical support, I thank James Rucker, Patricia Rucker, Edmund Mulaire, Kira Shepard, Ruth Hammen, and Leni Bowen.

Many of the ideas developed here originated in, or were sharpened by, discussions in the Propositional Attitudes Task Force, prominently including Merry Bergmann, G. Lee Bowie, John Connolly, Willem A. de Vries, Murray Kiteley, Meredith Michaels, Andrews Reath, Kenneth Taylor, and Tom Tymoczko. For especially close and critical readings of the text, and for innumerable suggestions, most of which have been incorporated, I thank Michael Arbib, Lynne Rudder Baker, John Connolly, Willem de Vries, Dan Lloyd, William Lycan, Raimo Tuomela, and several anonymous readers for the Press. I wish to note especially the valuable comments provided in lengthy conversations with Bill de Vries, John Connolly, Dan Lloyd, and Raimo Tuomela. These good friends deserve much of the credit for whatever is good in this book (and, needless to say, none of the blame for what is not). I also owe much to Wilfrid Sellars, whose great influence on my own thought is obvious.

I have also benefited from useful interchanges concerning these and related ideas with Timo Airaksinen, Bo Dahlbom, Bill Lycan, David Rosenbaum, Steve Weisler, and Chris Witherspoon, as well as other colleagues and students in the School of Communications and Cognitive Science at Hampshire College. I thank that school for providing the best possible environment for teaching and pursuing research in cognitive science, and Ruth Hammen for making the school possible.

Finally, I owe a great deal to my family—Blairie Garson (to whom I dedicate this study), Jonas Garson, Joshua Garfield, and Abraham Garfield —all of whom have had to put up with far more of my anxiety and with far less of me than they deserved. Saying thanks here is even less adequate in this case than in those above.

Belief in Psychology

Chapter 1
Introduction

Psychology—or at least the study of cognition—has, over the last twenty-five years, become increasingly dominated by computational approaches. Computational cognitive psychology is now probably the most salient branch of that science; it is the locus of a great deal of the most exciting psychological research, much as behavioristic learning theory was for the five preceding decades. This version of cognitive psychology (cognitivism) has become so enmeshed with artificial intelligence, linguistics, neuroscience, and the relevant branches of philosophy in the new academic treaty organization known as cognitive science that a very substantial part of the contemporary study of human psychology is truthfully characterizable as the study of human information processing, that is, as a species of the study of information processing generally. Whether this development in psychology is for good or for ill it is too early to say. Though the progress in many areas (e.g. eye movement control in reading, low-level vision, syntactic processing) is encouraging, some areas of human performance (e.g. face recognition, concept formation, semantic representation) present stubborn opposition. Rather than ask about the promise or lack thereof of cognitivism in psychology, I propose to accept its status as the best game in town and to ask what implications its pursuit has for the ontology of mind. How does cognitivism force us to think about the nature of psychological phenomena?

To get a feeling for the force of this question, consider a puzzle posed by two tales of mythical heroes of recent philosophical work on the foundations of cognitive science, Mary and Mr. Binh. Pylyshyn considers Mary's behavior in escaping a burning building:

> It simply will not do as an explanation of, say, why Mary came running out of a certain smoke-filled building, to say that there was a certain sequence of expressions computed in her mind according to certain expression-transforming rules. However true that might be, it fails on a number of counts to provide an explanation of Mary's behavior. It does not show how or why this behavior is related to very similar behavior she would exhibit as a result of receiving a

phone call in which she heard the utterance "this building is on fire!", or as a consequence of her hearing the fire alarm, or smelling smoke, or in fact following any event interpretable as generally entailing that the building was on fire. The only way to both capture the important underlying generalizations ... is to ... [interpret] the expressions in the theory as goals and beliefs. ...

Of course the computational [methodologically solipsistic] model only contains uninterpreted formal symbols. ... The question is whether the cognitive theory which that model instantiates can refrain from giving them an intentional [meaningful] interpretation. In the above example, leaving them as uninterpreted formal symbols simply begs the question of why these particular expressions should arise under what would surely seem (in the absence of interpretation) like a very strange collection of diverse circumstances, as well as the question of why these symbols should lead to building evacuation as opposed to something else. ... What is common to all of these situations is that a common interpretation of the events occurs. ... But what in the theory corresponds to this common interpretation? Surely one cannot answer by pointing to some formal symbols. *The right answer has to be something like the claim that the symbols represent the belief that the building is on fire.* ... (Pylyshyn 1980, p. 161; emphasis mine)

This last claim at least appears to be overwhelmingly plausible. Surely the proximal cause of Mary's hurried exit—whatever it is—has *that* causal power because it is (or at least represents) the belief that the building is on fire. Taking this view seriously, of course, commits us to the position that among the states that play explanatory roles in computational cognitive psychology will be such states as beliefs and the other propositional attitudes. In turn, this claim entails that mental phenomena will be individuated by reference to their content, and hence that more than the mere "syntax" of mental representations will be of concern to psychology. But consider Stich's discussion of Mr. Binh, "a recent immigrant to the United States whose mastery of English is rather shaky":

A bright and attentive man, Binh is anxious to learn as much as possible about his adopted country. On his first day off the plane, he overhears a conversation about a Mr. Jefferson, whose exploits are of obvious interest to the people on whom he is eavesdropping. Unknown to Binh, the people whose conversation he overhears are avid TV fans, and they are discussing the most recent travails of the fictional black dry-cleaning magnate. ... Binh takes it all in. The next day, Binh begins citizenship classes and he hears that Jefferson was a statesman, an inventor, and a major figure in the early history of America. Binh remembers, though he does not suspect that his teacher may be referring to a different Jefferson. On the third day Binh hears some discussion of a Mr. Feferman, a brilliant logician. However, with his ear not yet well attuned to spoken English, Binh hears "Feferman" as "Jefferson." Finally, on the fourth day, Binh meets an old friend and has a long chat about what he has learned of his new country. "I am," he says, "very anxious to learn more about this fascinating fellow Jefferson, the black patriot and statesman who made significant contributions to logic while building a dry-cleaning empire." (Stich 1983, pp. 145–146)

Recall the moral we just drew from our discussion of Mary: Among our psychological states are beliefs, and they are individuated by their content, that is, by what they are about. What made Mary's internal state so efficacious in her exit was the fact that it was *about fire*, and an adequate psychological explanation of her behavior would describe that state as a *belief about fire*. But what, or who, is poor Mr. Binh's psychological state—his desire—about? There is, of course no convenient referent who happens to satisfy the description "black patriot and statesman who made significant contributions to logic while building a dry-cleaning empire" as there is a convenient fire to fill in as the content for Mary's belief. And any good argument for suggesting that the desire is really about one of the three candidate referents can be met by equally good (or equally bad) arguments in support of either of the other two as the real referent. Perhaps it is about nothing. But that can't be—though Binh's desire is peculiar, from our perspective, it surely is not meaningless, since it is quite reasonable from his perspective.

The plausible moral that Stich draws from the case of Mr. Binh is that there just is no fact of the matter about what Mr. Binh's belief is about, and hence no fact of the matter about what its content is. So, although Mr. Binh surely harbors some psychological state to which we refer in our story, that state—which causes his utterance just as surely as Mary's belief causes her running—is not one that can be unequivocally characterized by reference to content. But if this is true, argue Stich and other doxastophobes in the cognitive-science community, then, in virtue of the fact that there is no psychologically interesting difference between Mr. Binh's desire and any of ours, the further moral to be drawn is that cognitive phenomena, insofar as they are described for the purposes of psychological explanation, cannot be characterized by reference to their content.

These two plausible morals are, obviously, contradictory. It can't be both that psychological explanations *must*, as Pylyshyn would have it, advert to content characterizations of psychological phenomena and, as Stich would have it, that they *can't*. This apparent antinomy poses the problem with which I shall be concerned: What is the place, if any, of the propositional attitudes in a scientifically respectable cognitive psychology, and in a philosophy of mind that respects such a psychology? By the end of the investigation, if we are successful, we should be prepared to provide an account that will allow us to provide plausible and consistent descriptions of the states of both Mary and Mr. Binh. With this introduction to the problem in mind, let us begin.

Psychology stands in a relation to its natural subject matter that is unusual among the sciences. Arguments against the possibility of scientific psychology are offered in serious tones, and are taken seriously (Davidson 1970a). Imagine a similar argument against the possibility of chemistry. Some have doubted and still doubt that mental events, states, and processes (henceforth, often, *phenomena*, in order to avoid repeating an awkward locution) exist (Dennett 1971, 1982; Stich 1983; Churchland 1979, 1981). Doubts about the existence of physical, chemical, biological, or even economic phenomena, though not unheard of, are at least more metaphysically and epistemologically outré, and when voiced are voiced with considerably more technical hedging. To be sure, instrumentalism has been influential in philosophical accounts of other sciences (see especially Van Fraassen 1980), but rarely have instrumentalist-realist debates raged with such vigor as when the phenomena under consideration are psychological in nature. And never has anyone suggested that anything like privileged access or incorrigibility attaches to the objects of physical theory.

Finally, psychology is peculiar in that it seems bound to commonsense to a greater degree than the physical sciences. This is a matter of some dispute and of great complexity, and a matter to which we will turn in detail in subsequent chapters. But because of its importance and despite its complexity, it deserves a bit of elaboration here. Psychology, especially contemporary cognitive psychology, *prima facie*, trafficks in such goods as beliefs, desires, pains, cogitations, and other such phenomena with which we are so familiar through prolonged intimate acquaintance that we come to believe, truly or falsely, that we know their nature without the benefit of science. Indeed, proponents of privileged-access theories of our knowledge of psychological states and other latter-day Cartesians would urge that we know their nature with more immediacy and certainty than we know anything else. Commonsense or sophisticated armchair-philosophical truisms about psychological phenomena, including claims about the truth conditions of expressions containing the terms denoting them, the kinds of things that can have them, and the nature of their interrelations and instantiations are taken to be serious constraints on psychological theory (Burge 1979; Loar 1981; Lycan 1981; Dennett 1982; Cummins 1983; Stich 1983; Pylyshyn 1984). This situation, where what appears to be the most fundamental ontological and theoretical level of the science is held responsible to the views of the person on the street (perhaps an artifact of the youth of cognitive science, though I rather suspect that it has to do with the domain) contrasts with the case in contemporary chemistry or physics, where commonsense claims about what counts as a metal or about the ultimate composition of matter are taken as far less serious constraints on fundamental chemical or physical theory or their respective ontologies.

Whether psychology—in particular, contemporary cognitive psychology—can or should retain this allegiance to the world of everyday appearance has been a matter of considerable debate in the philosophical literature on cognitive science (Churchland 1979, 1981; Cummins 1983; Dennett 1982; Pylyshyn 1984; Stich 1983; Baker, forthcoming). At stake are both the autonomy of psychology in determining the shape of its own domain and ontology and the shape that domain and that ontology eventually assume. This question will be the focus of the present book. In particular, I will explore the ways in which the propositional attitudes can be explained, accommodated, or explained away in the paradigm of computational psychology.

I choose the propositional attitudes (henceforth PAs) because they represent a *prima facie* central yet problematic family of everyday psychological properties. The PAs are, at least pretheoretically, both relational and intentional (in the now familiar neo-Brentanian sense of *contentful* or directed upon an object (see Dennett 1969, 1971). They are at least apparently relational, because they connect their subjects (typically persons) with the proposition that is the object of the attitude (or, depending on one's account, with a sentence [Carnap 1947], a token of a sentence [Fodor 1981], a set [Montague 1979; Stalnaker 1979], a situation [Barwise and Perry 1983], or some other stand-in). The connections come in different styles: "belief", "desire", "hope", "fear", and the other PA verbs are English labels for the ordinary taxonomy of relations persons bear to propositions or their proxies.

Of course there are immediate questions to raise: Are these psychological states really relational? Are there really the kinds of things posited as potential relata? If so, which ones? Are there really propositional attitudes? If so, are they properly the subject of a scientific psychology? All these questions will be addressed below. For now, it will be enough to stake out the territory within which the inquiry will be conducted. I assume that folk psychology (in the sense of Stich 1983) recognizes the existence and the relational character of the PAs, note that at least some cognitive psychologists do also (Pylyshyn 1984; Johnson-Laird 1983), and promise to raise and answer all of the above interesting philosophical questions in what follows.

The PAs are also intentional. This might appear in this context to be simply a way of being relational, but it is not. The intentionality of PAs indeed derives from their relation of persons to objects. But there are plenty of nonintentional relations that persons bear to objects (e.g. *being-to-the-left-of*), and even to propositions (e.g. *being-more-interesting-than*). Rather, what makes PAs intentional is that the relations between persons and propositions they comprise are intentional relations. The proposition toward which one has an attitude is, in some sense that is hard to specify, the *content* of one's mental state, and through this propositional content the subject of the attitude is related to "what the proposition is about." And it is this contentfulness, and the consequent directedness of the psychological state upon the world, that is the essence of intentionality. Another way of putting this is to say that PAs are *representational*. This is not a theoretical commonplace (see Searle 1980 for an opposing view), but the debates on the connection between intentionality and representation can be left aside for now.

Just what it is for a phenomenon to be representational will be considered below. (Qualia, by contrast, are—in folk psychology, anyway—monadic rather than relational, and, though psychological, are nonrepresentational. Qualia are the "feels" of phenomena—*what it is like to taste chocolate*, or *the experience of seeing green*. Qualia don't seem to be complex in the way that PAs are, though they may well have a complexity all their own [Dennett 1978b; Lycan 1983]. They don't resolve into anything like attitude and content. They don't seem to represent or to be about anything.)

Thus, the investigation has three aims. In the first place, as I have suggested in the preceding discussion, I am concerned specifically with understanding the ontology of computational psychology, and the ontology of mind that would be entailed by its success. That is, I intend to determine to what extent, and how, the psychological phenomena posited by folk psychology such as the PAs will be represented and explained by contemporary scientific psychology, and to what extent the success of computational psychology in accommodating them would alter our conception of their nature and properties, or its failure would impugn their reality or the adequacy of cognitive psychology.

The last remark connects directly to my next concern, which is a more general problem in the philosophy of science. This is the nature of the connection between the ontology of science and the ontology of what Sellars (1963) called the "manifest image of man-in-the-world." Is the role of science, as Sellars suggested, to provide an ontology and an image of the world that will ultimately supplant the manifest image, or is science (or at least some science—perhaps the social sciences) constrained in its ontology by the resources of the manifest image? The relationship between this question and those specifically about the place of the PAs in psychology in this study is twofold: On the one hand, an initial view on the more general question is a necessary precursor of the arguments I will advance concerning the more specific issues pertaining to the ontology of psychology and mind. On the other, the questions I raise about psychology are intended to serve as a case study to illustrate the view I will defend about the relation between the scientific and the manifest image.

Finally, in addition to these questions in the philosophy of science and the philosophy of psychology, I intend to make some progress toward the solution of ontological problems in the philosophy of mind—specifically, to get an account of the ontological supervenience base (Garfield 1983; Haugeland 1982; Kim 1978; Helman and Thompson 1975, 1976) of psychological phenomena. Getting clear about this matter will be a necessary component in the development of the argument concerning the place of these phenomena in psychology, as well as in the larger argument concerning the connection between science and the manifest image. The three goals are hence tightly interwoven, but I will disentangle them as much as possible at appropriate points in the argument.

The book is organized as follows: The groundwork for the investigation will be undertaken in chapters 2 and 3. In chapter 2 I will discuss some foundational issues in the philosophy of science. The aims will be to sketch a preliminary thesis about the relationship between the manifest and the scientific image and to locate psychological and computational phenomena within each image. Along the way, it will be necessary to address intertheoretic reduction and the nature of scientific domains. In chapter 3 I will examine the computational paradigm, detailing the nature of cognitive explanation, the role of the computer metaphor in cognitive psychology, and the nature and variety of functionalist theories of mind inspired thereby.

Chapters 4–7 make up the principal portion of the investigation. In chapter 4 I introduce the *prima facie* problems the PAs pose for computational psychology—problems that derive from their relational and intentional character—and the difficulties a purely computational account has in capturing all the features that appear to be essential to this character. I then introduce the four principal approaches to surmounting these problems: Methodological Solipsism, Naturalistic Individualism, Eliminative Computationalism, and Eliminative Materialism.

Methodological Solipsism and Naturalistic Individualism both attempt to accommodate the PAs within the cognitive paradigm. They are reconciliationist attempts at solution, though the methodological solipsist holds out hope of capturing far less of the pretheoretic concept of a propositional attitude, such as belief, in a scientific psychology than the naturalistic individualist.

Eliminative Computationalism and Eliminative Materialism are the two eliminativist alternatives. Each solves the problem by denying the existence of the PAs. They differ, however, both in the source and in nature of their nihilism. The eliminative computationalist argues that the triumph of the computational paradigm is imminent, and that there is no room in it for anything resembling a PA, and consequently, that there is no such thing as belief, or any other PA. The eliminative materialist, on the other hand, argues that the computational paradigm is ultimately bankrupt, in part because it is committed to the reality of something like the PAs, and that both computationalism and the PAs are destined for the scrapheap of discarded theories and discarded theoretical entities.

Chapters 5 and 6 show why the reconciliationist and the eliminativist theory are wrong. I argue that the reconciliationist strategies fail because each of them ultimately presupposes what I call (following Burge [1979, 1982, 1987]; see Garfield 1983) an individualist theory of meaning for psychological phenomena. I argue that no such theory can adequately characterize intentional phenomena. I propose two distinct arguments against the eliminativist strategy: that it mistakes the relationship between the scientific and manifest images, giving too much ontological authority to science, and that, if the strategy were true, assertions of its truth would have no content.

Chapter 7 offers my own positive proposal concerning the nature of the PAs, their place in psychology, and the implications of this view for the nature of psychology and the relation between the view of persons generated by a successful scientific psychology and that offered by the manifest image of man-in-the-world. I argue for a naturalistic, socio-culturally sensitive construal of psychological phenomena, and for a correspondingly naturalistic approach to psychology. I will suggest that the manifest image places constraints on the domain of psychology through its preoccupation (shared by other social and behavioral sciences) with phenomena constituted by persons embedded within cultures that construct the manifest image, and that these constraints issue in the incoherence of any account of intentional states that either denies their existence or does serious violence to their relational, intentional character and to their kinship with linguistic states.

The conclusions I reach about the ontological status of representational phenomena such as the PAs and about the shape of psychological theory diverge sharply from standard philosophical accounts. However, I will argue, they are in great harmony with current trends in research in the cognitive-science paradigm, and hence they represent no prescription for significant change in the conduct of the psychological enterprise within that tradition, though these conclusions do call for a reconceptualization of the enterprise.

Chapter 2

Metascientific Preliminaries

My principal concern in this chapter is to get clear about the foundational issues pertinent to the identification of the proper domain of cognitive psychology and about the connections between this domain and the ontology of the manifest image. I will begin by discussing the nature of theoretical domains generally, with an emphasis on the domain of psychology, and follow with a discussion of intertheoretic reduction, of the implications of such reduction for the distinctions between theoretical domains, and of the potential collapse of such distinctions. The second half of the chapter will be devoted to the relation between the manifest and scientific images and to the location of folk-psychological and computational states within these images.

A brief catalog of the sciences now recognized in ordinary academic discourse and a moment's theoretical reflection should suffice to convince one that there is nothing immutable, necessary, or even, in any strong sense, principled about the taxonomy of scientific domains. The domains of astronomy, physics, chemistry, molecular biology, evolutionary biology, ethology, neuroscience, linguistics, psychology, sociology, economics, and political science seem to grade off into one another on a continuum. If anything, the proliferation of subdisciplines and interdisciplines only enhances this sense of continuity. It would be odd, however, to assert that the domains of economics and particle physics (to take examples at the extremes) are coincident, or even intersecting.

There is, of course, nothing paradoxical here. The domain of a science comprises just what a science takes as its objects of study, and typically, for any interesting object of study, it is true that several relatively contiguous sciences, but not all sciences, will have something to say about it. Thus, both solid-state physics and organic chemistry have something to say about the aperiodic crystals that are fundamental to life, while neither has any interest in consumers' expected utility estimation algorithms, which are of interest to both psychologists and economists.

Aside from the fact that the boundaries between domains are typically fuzzy and the fact that domains are typically intersecting, domains and their boundaries are also malleable. Heredity was not a concern of organic chemistry before the requisite advances in cellular biology. Before the work of Broca, Wernicke, and later Chomsky and his followers, human language was not part of the domain of biology or neuroscience. There are instances of contraction as well; the study of the reflex arc has moved from psychology to neuroscience, as has the study of "blind sight" or tectal vision. But behind this malleability there may be a certain immutability at the core of the domain of any science—a range of phenomena which it cannot ignore on pain of evacuating itself and going out of business. If the world's physicists suddenly declared that the fundamental particles and forces of nature were no longer in the purview of physics, there would be a strong temptation to say that they had simply, en masse, decided to abdicate the enterprise of physics. Whether the domain of psychology possesses such an essential core, and what its contents (if any) are, are questions of central concern for this investigation. In order to answer them, however, we must first examine the survey by which psychology demarcates its boundaries.

Pylyshyn offers these observations:

> [There is the prospect that] cognitive science is a genuine scientific domain like the domains of chemistry, biology, economics, [and] geology. In scientific domains it is possible to develop theories based on a special vocabulary or reasonably uniform set of principles independent of the principles of other sciences—that is, principles with considerable autonomy.... Just as the domain of biology includes something like all living things (for which a strict definition is probably impossible outside of biological theory), so the domain of cognitive science may be something like "knowing things"....
>
> Humans are living things, and consequently advances in biological science will contribute to a fuller understanding of human nature. Similarly, because we are informavores, or cognizers, understanding human nature can also gain from the study of principles governing members of that domain. At the moment it appears that included in this category are the higher vertebrates and certain computer systems. In any case, in view of ... the impressive successes in recent work on artificial intelligence, one ought to take such a possibility seriously. (1984, pp. xi–xii)

Two suggestions regarding the domain of psychology emerge here. The first is a methodological point about the demarcation of domains: A domain is a range of phenomena (where this is neutral between objects, events, properties, states, processes, or any other ontological category) about which "it is possible to develop theories based on a special vocabulary or reasonably uniform set of principles" distinct from and independent of those appropriate to other domains. Domains are hence individuated not directly with reference to an arbitrary taxonomy of the things contained in them (living vs. nonliving, terrestrial vs. celestial, etc.), but rather with reference to the vocabularies and explanatory strategies appropriate to their investigation. The inventory of things in a domain is determined, in turn, by the limits of the successful application of these vocabularies and strategies. Domain individuation hence proceeds on pragmatic rather than ontological principles.

Such a pragmatic principle of individuation has certain advantages over an ontological approach. First, it can account for the intersection and the fuzziness of scientific domains. Even if one were committed to a theory- and language-independent ontological regimentation of the furniture of the world into categories, one could without embarrassment concede that there are often disparate vocabularies and explanatory strategies appropriate to the study of a single phenomenon, depending upon one's scientific interests. In addition, such a pragmatic principle can explain both how pairs of phenomena that appear to be quite unrelated (e.g. computing machinery and people) can find themselves within the same theoretical domain while pairs that seem quite closely related fall for some purposes in distinct theoretical domains (e.g. reflexes and centrally controlled movements, which for fifty years were in the same domain).

The second, more substantive claim that Pylyshyn makes in the above-quoted paragraphs is that the vocabulary and explanatory principles that stake out the domain of cognitive science are those appropriate to "informavores, or cognizers"—that is, information-processing systems. Just what this entails, and how far psychology can take this as a specification of its domain, will emerge in subsequent chapters.

Recognizing the pragmatic nature of domain specification raises the prospect—a significant one for psychology—that what one thinks to be a domain is in fact not one, and hence that one's scientific enterprise—not one specific theory or hypothesis, but one's entire paradigm—may turn out to be a blind alley. The reason for this is that, on a pragmatic individuation principle, a domain comprises just what is successfully described by a particular theoretical vocabulary and explained by a particular set of generalizations, laws, or other theoretical apparatus. (See Cummins 1983 for a useful taxonomy of explanatory strategies.) But theoretical vocabulary and explanations are themselves dependent for their sense and their utility on the theories in the context of which they occur. And theories sometimes turn out to be false. A radically false theory could render a significant portion of the vocabulary and the explanatory apparatus thought to constitute a domain senseless and useless. Pylyshyn (1984, p. 264) is aware of this hazard: "All of this should alert us both to the possibility that we are on the wrong track—there might be no natural explanatory domain of cognition—and that, even if there is such a domain, we may be wrong in several of our pretheoretical intuitions about it. One of the things we are most likely to be wrong about, judging from what has happened in other disciplines, are the boundaries of the domain."

The second hazard to which Pylyshyn alludes is a less drastic version of the first, though it is not so benign as it might appear. At the least, such "boundary error" could mean that one or two phenomena that one thought were on one side of the domain boundary could fall on the other. For instance, one might be surprised to learn that cardiac regulation can be usefully described and explained as a cognitive process, or that certain kinds of aphasia cannot. But what if it turned out that one of the most central phenomena that we think, pretheoretically, lies within the heart of a domain turns out not to be fruitfully described or explained in terms of the apparatus of that domain? Suppose that were true of all, or nearly all, of the intentional states recognized by folk psychology? At such a point one would be faced with the choice between jettisoning the offending phenomena from the purview of the science, thus doing violence to common-sense, and dramatically revising the conduct of one's science. We will encounter arguments in subsequent chapters that claim that this is just the situation in which the computational paradigm finds itself. Hence, a strategy for resolving dilemmas of this type will be necessary.

Theoretical domains and their boundaries are constantly in danger from another quarter as well: The entities and principles governing a domain may become superfluous as a consequence of intertheoretic reduction. It is to this topic that we now turn.

The philosophical literature on intertheoretic reduction in science is vast, and it would serve little purpose to survey it here. The points I wish to make are perfectly general with respect to major competing accounts, and so I will simply note that the model I endorse is that offered by Churchland (1979). On Churchland's view, the central features of successful theoretical reductions are the *displacement* of the reduced theory by the reducing theory and the *preservation* of an "equipotent image" of the reduced theory in the reducing theory.

Both displacement and preservation, in actual cases of reduction, are matters of degree. When a successor theory T_2 reduces a previously held theory T_1 in a domain, it does so in virtue of its greater explanatory power and scope. T_2 will in general serve at least as well as T_1 over the same range of phenomena, and will improve upon it both by solving problems or explaining phenomena that were within the scope of T_1 but were recalcitrant in the face of its theoretical resources and by being more general than T_1. This greater generality of T_2 typically emerges in two ways. One is that T_2 will typically explain a wider range of phenomena than did T_1. Second, and more important from the standpoint of reduction, T_2 will typically explain the success (typically, in light of the hypothesized reduction, a qualified success) enjoyed by T_1. This explanation of the qualified success of a predecessor theory makes what would otherwise be a mere theoretical displacement a theoretical reduction, and it is this aspect of reduction that is captured by the notion of the preservation of an equipotent image of T_1 in T_2.

The idea is this: T_1 and T_2 are theories. Each comprises a set of sentences, a set of rules of inference, and a set of theoretical terms. We can identify a rough set of "core theorems" of T_1, those predictions and theoretical claims that are central to T_1's explanatory success. In typical cases, some of these will be existence claims regarding important theoretical entities; some will be empirical predictions taken as confirmatory of the theoretical principles from which they follow; some will be correlations, and so on. They will certainly include the central theoretical principles of T_1. In a case where T_2 reduces T_1, these "core theorems" of T_1 will each (or at least most of them will, and this is one source of the "matter-of-degreeness" of reduction on this account) have a "twin," or a statement of nearly identical empirical content (the other source of matter-of-degree-ness) in the set of theorems of T_2.

With this account of theoretical reduction in hand, two points of interest to our investigation of the ontology of cognition need to be made. The first is that, on this model, reduction is defined as a relation between *theories*. To the extent that an account of a domain is not theoretical in a sense to be specified in the next section of this chapter, there is no sense in which it is a candidate for reduction to anything. The second point is that this account of theoretical reduction does not commit one to the claim that, when one theory reduces another, each theoretical posit of the reduced theory—or even *any* theoretical posit of the reduced theory—is shown to be identical with, or definable in terms of, items in the ontology of the reducing theory. So a reduction is possible in the absence of any "bridge laws" linking the predicates of the reducing theory with predicates of the reduced theory. Theoretical reduction is hence possible, even with the preservation of a substantial image of an old theory in the reducing theory, despite the wholesale replacement of the ontology of the reduced theory with a completely incommensurable and novel ontology in the reducing theory. And in general, this ontological revision is probably more the rule than the exception. But again, this says nothing about ontologies that may not be theoretical in nature.

Reduction is often vindication. To the extent that a more fundamental theory (e.g., physics or chemistry) has better scientific credentials (i.e., is better confirmed, more general, etc.) than a less fundamental theory (e.g., psychology or economics), a reduction of the latter to the former can lend credence to the less fundamental theory simply by demonstrating that it has an image in the epistemically sounder theory. But it in no way follows that the absence of such a reduction should be construed as an epistemic blot on a high-level theory. That would require a powerful argument for the unity of science—one that is unlikely to be forthcoming.

In "Philosophy and the Scientific Image of Man," Sellars (1960) distinguishes between the "Manifest Image of Man-In-The-World" and the "Scientific Image of Man-In-the World" (henceforth just the "scientific" and the "manifest" image). In this discussion I will embrace the distinction— indeed, I will defend a strong version of it against Sellars's own weakening (in the final sections of his essay) of the claim that the distinction necessitates a "binocular vision" and against Churchland's (1979) implicit attack on the reality of the manifest image.

"The manifest image," Sellars says, " ... is, first, the framework in terms of which man came to be aware of himself as man-in-the-world. It is the framework in terms of which ... man first encountered himself, which is, of course, when he came to be man. For it is no merely incidental feature of man that he has a conception of himself as man-in-the-world, just as it is obvious, on reflection, that 'if man had a radically different conception of himself he would be a radically different kind of man.'" (1960, p. 6) This is the manifest image in its first aspect: the image in which persons locate themselves as persons, and which determines the conceptual structure in which persons conceptualize themselves and the world in which they find themselves. It is an image arrived at pretheoretically, but is not on that account a "primitive" image pervaded by superstition or misconception and demanding conceptual exorcism. (It does, however, contrast with a conceptually more primitive "original image" in which everything is conceived as personal. But again, that image need not be considered on that account superstitious.) It is, rather, the conceptual lens through which we, merely as a consequence of being the organisms we are, growing up in the cultures we grow up in, come to see ourselves and the world of middle-sized dry goods we inhabit. But this characterization, while it tells us what kind of thing the manifest image is, tells us little about its specific content. This is the second aspect of its characterization:

> ... we are approaching an answer to the question, "What are the basic objects of the manifest image?" when we say that it includes persons, animals, lower forms of life and "merely material" things, like rivers and stones....
>
> The first point I wish to make is that there is an important sense in which the primary objects of the manifest image are *persons*. And to understand how this is so, is to understand central, and, indeed, crucial themes in the history of philosophy. Perhaps the best way to make the point is to refer back to the construct which we called the "original" image of man-in-the-world, and characterize it as a frame-

work in which *all* of the "objects" are persons. From this point of view, the refinement of the "original" image into the manifest image, is the gradual "de-personalization" of objects other than persons.... Even persons, it is said (mistakenly, I believe), are being "de-personalized" by the advance of the scientific point of view. (Sellars 1960, pp. 9–10)

This begins to characterize the ontology of the manifest image, and to explain why it is the image in terms of which persons first (in both a temporal and a conceptual sense) experience themselves as persons in a world. When we see the world as it manifests itself to us (this turn of phrase is somewhat misleading—it sounds as though the world is actively "manifesting," while we are passive receivers of manifestation—rather, the idea is that of the world as we spontaneously, though actively, represent it), it is a world in which we humans alone qualify as persons, and in which we are surrounded by tables, chairs, dogs, cats, and the rest of the familiar furniture of our everyday ontology.

I suggested that this image is prior to the scientific image (yet to be elaborated) in both a temporal and a conceptual sense (ignoring for a moment the historical priority of the original image, which doesn't concern us here). The temporal sense is the more straightforward of the two. The conceptual resources required to represent the objects and relations of the manifest image are those embedded in our cultures and our languages. As we learn to speak and to think, as we learn the predicates and nouns of our language, we acquire the fundamental ontology of our culture, and hence the manifest image. It is only later, if at all, that we learn to theorize, to do science, and hence to conceive of the world and of our situation therein in the language and the categories of science. (Of course one might argue, and Churchland [1979] does, that this needn't be the case—that one could, and indeed that someday people will, be brought up in the scientific image. However, this requires considerable argument—argument which I will explore below, only to argue in later chapters that it is blocked by the conceptual priority of the manifest image, to which we now turn.)

... the essentially social character of conceptual thinking comes clearly to mind when we recognize that there is no thinking apart from common standards of correctness and relevance, which relate what *I do* think to what *anyone ought to* think. The contrast between I and "anyone" is essential to rational thought....

The manifest image must, therefore, be construed as containing a conception of itself as a group phenomenon, the group mediating between the individual and the intelligible order. (Sellars 1960, pp. 16–17)

It is in the manifest image that persons, norms, rules of meaning, relevance, and reason are to be found. Thus, on this account, it is only by participating in the manifest image as a member of a group, as a follower of epistemic and linguistic rules, and hence as a person that one can engage in the sophisticated representational activity, hypothesis construction, and theorizing that makes science and hence the scientific image possible. Indeed, language itself—the vehicle of science and (as I will argue) the model and foundation of conceptual thought—has its necessary conditions in the manifest image.

But while the manifest image is the image in which we must find ourselves in order to be able to engage in the scientific enterprise, it poses problems of explanation and understanding that are incapable of solution within its own conceptual and ontological resources. It is these problems that provide the stimulus to science and the scientific image. The scientific image is the image of the world that includes, not the persons, communities, dogs, cats, tables, chairs, and other middle-sized perceptibles that make up the manifest image, but the theoretical entities—particles, forces, magnitudes, and quantitative relationships—that theoretical science employs to, in part, explain the nature and behavior of the objects in the manifest image.

The scientific image, of course, is both complex and evolving. Its complexity issues from the fact that it is constituted not by one unified science but by a plethora of partially overlapping sciences, each introducing its own ontology and its own way of ordering the phenomena in its purview. It hence presents itself as a kaleidoscopic (more accurately, a cubist) image of the world, but one that is perhaps resolving itself into more congruent, if not fewer, facets, as the several sciences that co-constitute it evolve. Its evolution is irregular, with an ontology that expands and contracts without warning, losing phlogiston here, gaining an intermediate boson there, losing an operant, gaining a short-term memory register. But the evolution is, overall, progressive: More phenomena are explained and ordered within the scientific image over time, and, in general, the extensions of the sets of successfully explained phenomena are conservative.

Before we turn to the complex and strained relationship between the two images, it is worth noting that the manifest image is not as static as my characterization might have suggested, but is, like the scientific image, in a state of flux. Indeed, and this is a critical aspect of the relationship between the images, the flux of the manifest image is in part a function of the evolution and assimilation of the scientific image into popular culture. Whereas once we perceived stars as rotating around the Earth in a celestial sphere, this apparent rotation, after its explanation by the theoretical apparatus of Copernican astronomy, drops from our image of the world, and we instead perceive the motion of the Earth around the Sun and its changing orientation with respect to the relatively stationary stellar background. This point—that our perception is wonderfully plastic in response to our background knowledge—is made eloquently in chapter 2 of Churchland 1979, and we will return to it in much more detail below. For now, it is enough to note that the manifest image not only poses problems for science but itself subtly alters in response to the demands placed upon it by the answers returned.

The relation between the scientific and the manifest image is, as I just mentioned, uneasy:

> The fact that each theoretical image is a construction on a foundation provided by the manifest image, and *in this methodological sense* presupposes the manifest image, makes it tempting to suppose that the manifest image is prior in a *substantive* sense; that the categories of a theoretical science are logically dependent on categories ... in the manifest world.... Yet, when we turn ... to "the" scientific image ..., we note that although the image is *methodologically* dependent on the world of sophisticated common sense ... it purports to be a *complete* image, i.e., to define a framework which could be the *whole truth* about that which belongs to the image.... [T]he scientific image presents itself as a *rival* image. From its point of view the manifest image on which it rests is an "inadequate" but pragmatically useful likeness of a reality which first finds its adequate ... likeness in the scientific image....
>
> To all of which, of course, the manifest image, or, more accurately, the perennial philosophy which endorses its claims, replies that the scientific image cannot replace the manifest without rejecting its own foundation. (Sellars 1960, pp. 20–21)

The problem is that what appears to be a desirable binocular or stereoscopic vision of the world, provided by the synopsis of the two images, is constantly threatened by the hegemonist tendencies of the scientific image. While the manifest image reveals the world to us as it appears to (relatively) naive perception, a view codified by the sophisticated philosophy of common sense, the scientific image purports to reveal the world as it really is. At its best, the plasticity of perception is, from the standpoint of the scientific image, the ability of our perceptual and commonsense epistemic categories to adapt to the deliverances of the scientific image; at its worst, it is the possibility of the mendacious deformation of the world as it is by doxastically infected receptivity. The scientific image, on the other hand, claims for itself not so much plasticity as evolutionary convergence to the truth. On this account, the manifest/scientific distinction is tantamount to, or at least approaching, the classical appearance/reality distinction.

The manifest image, on the other hand, claims a certain indispensability. For one thing, no matter how superior the categories of science are in point of their empirical adequacy to the fine structure of reality, their origins are in the categories of the manifest image. They are extended refinements of the ordinary categories of objects, forces, actions, relations, and properties. Hence, while the scientific categories may kick away their commonsense ladder, it is a ladder they were nonetheless forced to climb, and which we, in coming to see the world from the sophisticated vantage point of science, must climb as well.

What is more, claims the manifest image, the natural and ultimate explananda of science are the phenomena in the manifest image that pose the questions to which science provides the answer. Ultimately we live in the manifest image by force, as a consequence of our native perceptual and epistemic endowment, and adopt science by choice in order to deepen and refine our understanding of this world. Without the manifest image, science loses both its raison d'être and its meaningfulness as an activity.

Finally (and, as we shall see below, most importantly), it is in the manifest image that we find persons. The scientific image is a depersonalization of the manifest image just as the manifest image is a depersonalization of the original image. The briefest way to put the point is this: The concept of a person is the concept of a thing that, at least, conforms its cognitive and linguistic behavior, and its other social behavior as well, to rules, and does so in the context of a community that is capable of articulating and enforcing these rules. A central feature of persons, then, is the normative character of the predicables appropriate to them, and it is of the essence of the scientific image that its predicables are descriptive rather than normative.

Given this tension between (or what Sellars calls a "clash of") the images, four kinds of resolution appear, at first glance, possible: (1) The scientific image could vanquish the manifest image, and we could come to see the manifest image as a legacy of a primitive past, on a continuum with the original image. (2) The manifest image could vanquish the scientific image, and we could come to see the scientific image as a mere calculational instrument for effective prediction, control, and explanation of manifest phenomena. (3) The images could both be retained, in a binocular approach to the conception of man-in-the-world. (4) A synthesis could be achieved between the images, resolving them into a single image of man-in-the-world incorporating essential features of each.

The second alternative—the elimination of the scientific image from our view of the world and the concomitant relegation of all science to an instrumental status—seems the only genuine noncontender among these alternatives. This is not the place to delve into the extensive literature concerning the realism/instrumentalism issue in the interpretation of scientific theories. I will simply assert that the claims of science to truth as opposed to mere instrumental success are too strong, and the place of science in the enterprise of constructing our collective understanding of the nature of reality is too central, to allow the suggestion that it can be subordinated this dramatically in an account of our knowledge of the world.

Of the remaining three views (which I will dub the scientist, the binocular, and the synthetic, respectively), Sellars argues for the synthetic, Churchland (1979) for the scientist, and I will eventually defend a version of the binocular.

Sellars argues for a synthesis of the images in which the scientific is primary but in which persons are accommodated by an understanding of normative properties achieved by embedding these properties (and consequently persons, who are their primary bearers) in the scientific image. The mediating link, and the primary subject of this study, is the embedding of such states as beliefs in the scientific image through their identification with neurophysiological states.

The central components of the synthesis are the familiar Sellarsian accounts (developed in more detail in Sellars 1956, 1974, 1980, and 1981) of linguistic meaning and of the linguistic model of mental events. Sellars argues that the meaning of linguistic items is to be understood in terms of the functional roles they play in linguistic practice. On this account, "means" is analyzed as a special form of the copula, where " 'Φ' means Ψ" is analyzed as " 'Φ' is a $\cdot\Psi\cdot$", and "$\cdot\Psi\cdot$" is an expression that denotes any expression that plays the same role in its language that "Ψ" plays in its language. Now, the second stage in the account consists in noting that for Sellars a thought that Θ just is some psychological state that is a $\cdot\Theta\cdot$, that is, some state that plays the same role in the subject's internal psychological economy that 'Θ' plays in natural language. And finally, Sellars claims, the states that are the candidates in the scientific image for the functional equivalents in the internal economies of believers of linguistic items in public language are events in the central nervous system described in the language of neurophysiology.

The final stage of the Sellarsian synthesis of the images is one Sellars sketches only in the most general terms. The idea is that once individual thoughts, intentions, and other psychological phenomena are understood on the account sketched in the preceding paragraph, a theory of group or community intentions, and hence an account of the rules and norms the applicability of which is definitive of personhood, can be developed. Hence, the argument concludes, the framework of persons, the manifest image, need not be jettisoned but can be accommodated within the scientific image. In such a synthesis, beings can be understood to possess normative

properties in virtue of their naturalistic relations to naturalistically characterized community intentions (see, e.g., Tuomela 1985).

Before turning to Churchland's darker view of the future of the manifest
image, I want to offer two comments on Sellars's account, both of which
will be developed in much more detail in subsequent chapters. Though I
will adopt a view of the individuation of psychological phenomena that is
very much in the spirit of Sellars's account, I will part company with him
when it comes to identifying neurophysiological phenomena as the tokens
whose roles are to be identified with those of public linguistic tokens. I will
adopt a view according to which psychological states are more broadly
supervenient than this. (The interested reader may skip to chapters 5 and 7
for this account.) Second, though rejecting Sellars's argument for the unifi-
cation of the images, and arguing for an account whereby the manifest
image and the scientific image stand as mutually necessary but distinct
lenses through which we represent the world, I will embrace a view very
much like that Sellars sketches at the end of "Philosophy and the Scientific
Image of Man" according to which a psychology that does justice to the
PAs will of necessity be one that takes seriously the normative embedding
of persons in their communities.

Although in *Scientific Realism and the Plasticity of Mind* Churchland does not
acknowledge that he has set out to demonstrate the inevitability of the
demise of the manifest image, his account of the nature and the fate of our
everyday notions of persons, psychological phenomena, and the framework in which we currently conceptualize the world and ourselves directly
entails such a view. The argument begins with a Sellarsian observation
about the nature of perceptual consciousness and the fixation of perceptual
belief:

> The guiding conviction ... is as follows: *perception consists in the
> conceptual exploitation of the natural information contained in our sensa-
> tions or sensory states.* ... [I]t suggests a question: how efficient are we
> at exploiting this information? The answer ... is that we are not very
> efficient as it, or rather, not nearly as efficient as we might be. ...
>   ... Our current modes of conceptual exploitation are rooted, in
> substantial measure, not in the nature of our perceptual environment,
> nor in the innate features of our psychology, but rather in the struc-
> ture and content of our common language. ... [E]ach of us grows into
> a conformity with the current conceptual template. In large measure
> we *learn*, from others, to perceive the world as everyone else per-
> ceives it. But if this is so, then we might have learned, and may yet
> learn, to conceive/perceive the world in ways other than those
> supplied by our present culture. ...
>   The obvious candidate here is the conceptual framework of modern

physical theory—of physics, chemistry, and their many satellite sciences. That the conceptual framework of these sciences is immensely powerful is beyond argument, and its credentials as a systematic representation of reality are unparalleled. (Churchland 1979, p. 6)

The argument that Churchland sketches here and develops at much greater length in chapters 2 and 4 of his book runs as follows: Our perceptual beliefs, including our introspective judgments about our own qualitative and intentional phenomena, are not inevitable consequences of our peripheral or endogenous stimulation. Rather, they are interpretations of the "readings" of our sensory and introspective "meters." (It is, of course, an interesting epistemological question—though not one with which we will concern ourselves in this study—just what the status of these "introspective meter readings" are in light of Churchland's professed rejection of the "myth of the given." It is not at all clear that this story can be told coherently.) Our senses (including introspection) react to the energies that impinge upon them by rather reliably entering certain states. In order to get from these caused states to belief, however, we must *interpret* the states of our senses. So, when we judge, say, that we are seeing a patch of maroon in the center of the visual field, or that we are experiencing a pounding headache in the left temple, or that we believe that snow is white, we infer from the states of the relevant sensory organs that there is a patch, from our proprioceptive neural feedback that we are in pain, and from slightly different monitoring of our current neurophysiological state that we have the belief.

But, the argument continues, there must be premises mediating the inference from nonconceptual sensory state to perceptual belief. These premises must derive from some theory about the structure of the world, the structure of our epistemic apparatus, and the constitution of our sensory organs, just as the inference from the readings on the meters attached to a linear accelerator to the belief that they are registering the emission of a particular microphysical particle is mediated by current physical theory and by a theory about the operation of the accelerator and the instruments being read. What is the theory that commonly mediates the inferences that issue in our everyday perceptual beliefs? It is, of course, none other than the commonsense view of the nature of the world and of ourselves, a theory embodied in the manifest image.

There are, however, Churchland argues, two things terribly wrong with this commonsense theory. In the first place, it is not a fine-grained enough theory of the nature of our sensory apparatus. Our eyes and ears, for instance, are sensitive to the wavelengths of incoming light, to reflectivities of surfaces, to the wavelengths and amplitudes of ambient sound waves. In fixing our perceptual beliefs, we ignore most of this information in favor of a more coarse-grained taxonomy of colors and notes. Our introspective faculties are sensitive to the frequencies of neural firings and concentrations of neuro-transmitters in highly localized portions of the central nervous system. We reject this information in favor of a coarse taxonomy of headaches, itches, and the like. But the theory, on this account, is more radically flawed still. Churchland argues that much of this commonsense "theory"—from everyday physics untutored by the general-relativistic quantum theory to commonsense psychology untutored by a well-developed neuroscience—is false. We know it to be false because it diverges from the articulated sciences, which are more successful in explanation and prediction over the same domains.

The upshot is that the world we perceive, with its medium-sized dry goods, its persons, and its familiar psychological phenomena, is a poor substitute for the world we could be perceiving if only our perceptual beliefs were inferred from our sensory states according to premises supplied to us by the true science. But there is hope, because perception is plastic! After all, we learned the false theory we currently use to generate our false representation of reality. Surely we could learn the true theory and put it to use representing reality correctly, hence coming to "directly" perceive, in the same sense in which we directly perceive our current battery of perceptibles—that is, spontaneously generate perceptual beliefs in response to peripheral stimulation via premises from our theory at hand—an accurate theory of the fine structure of the world, or at least that portion of it to which our sensory apparatus is differentially sensitive.

At this stage, we are close to the conclusion that the manifest image will vanish. We are at least assured, if Churchland is correct to this point, that the manifest image will undergo dramatic transformation. But what remains is for Churchland to argue that the central feature of the manifest image— persons, and with them normative properties—will vanish as well. The argument here relies on the claim that persons, their intentional and qualitative properties, and all else that goes along with them, are elements of the ontology of what Churchland calls the P-theory—the commonsense theory of such things. But its predictive and explanatory power, he argues, and its grain, pale beside those of a finished neurophysiology, and it finds no remotely equipotent image in any plausible version of a finished neuroscience. Hence, it is false. Hence the objects and processes it posits as its theoretical entities do not exist. Hence, the manifest image is an illusion which we will be better off shedding.

A good deal of chapters 5–7 will be devoted to showing why neither this nihilistic attack on the manifest image nor even Sellars's assimilationist approach to it can work—to showing that the manifest image makes independent ontological claims upon us and upon the ontology of a psychology of persons. Now it is important to bear in mind the structure of these attacks on the independence of that image, for both will be represented in the discussion of the place of the PAs in psychology to follow. The one approach proceeds by embedding the problematic components of the manifest image in science and then salvaging them by reduction to ontologically secure elements of the scientific image; the other proceeds by arguing that the manifest image is scientific in the first place, but that it constitutes bad science and so can make no ontological claims on us. Before moving on to a characterization of the computational paradigm in psychology, I want to discuss the place of the PAs and their putative theoretical counterpart, computational states in the manifest and scientific images.

The PAs seem at first glance to be firmly entrenched in the manifest image. To be sure, Churchland (1979) and Stich (1983) argue that they are in fact the theoretical entities of woefully false scientific theories, while Pylyshyn (1984) argues that they find natural counterparts in the theoretical entities of a possibly true psychological theory. But without such powerful (and problematic) philosophical arguments, to the relatively naive observer, such states as belief and seeing red appear to be among the properties that are accessible to spontaneous perception or introspection without the aid of theoretical reasoning and that are tied closely to the existence and the intellectual activity of persons and their ilk.

Thus, there are only two ways in which we could be convinced that there are no actual commonsense psychological phenomena located in the manifest image. We could be convinced, as Churchland would have it, that the manifest image is mere illusion, and that there are no such psychological states—that they are as mythical as phlogiston. Or we could be convinced, as Stich and Pylyshyn would have it, that these phenomena are theoretical entities postulated by a theory about how people work (for Stich a radically false one, for Pylyshyn an approximately true one). We have seen what the argument against the reality of the manifest image and its ontological furniture looks like. Let us examine for a moment the form of an argument for the theoretical status of the commonsense psychological phenomena.

We have already seen the argument in a different context in our discussion of Churchland's attack on the manifest image. The central intuition here, as there, is that our psychological phenomena and those of our fellows are not "given" to us directly in perception or introspection but are, rather, posited as a conceptual response to external or internal stimulation. The conceptual response has the form of spontaneous inference, and the premises that mediate the inference, as well as the entities postulated as responsible for the stimulations received, are components of a theory of how persons operate, of the causes of behavior and stimulation. (This point is made most forcefully in Sellars 1956.) Hence, even the ontology of commonsense psychology, which might appear to be of a status quite different from that of more obviously theoretical sciences, is to be understood as theoretical in form and therefore of a piece with the scientific image. It would follow from this line of argument that the same standards of epistemic and theoretical evaluation should be applied to this framework that should be applied to those frameworks we have always recognized to be scientific. (This is, of course, what Churchland and Stich do, and they find the commonsense framework wanting in differing ways and to differing degrees. Pylyshyn applies these standards as well, but he returns a different verdict.)

In chapter 7 I will argue that this view is ultimately mistaken, and that the manifest image, while indeed sharing certain key features with the scientific image, retains an independence of method and an independence of ontology that require the predicates applicable to persons to be treated somewhat specially. In particular, I will argue that the intentionality and the responsibility to communal norms of meaningful linguistic and psychological phenomena are presuppositions of the very possibility of the construction of the scientific image, and that they cannot be jettisoned on pain of evacuating the content of its theories. I will argue further that, given the nature of the domain of psychology, the ontology of the manifest image places special constraints on its theoretical entities and its methodology.

One final preliminary remark is in order before I embark upon a characterization of the computational psychology in which I am most directly interested: The fact that I will argue that the manifest framework makes prior ontological claims on many commonsense psychological phenomena in no way precludes the positing of more theoretical psychological events, states, and processes, which may in some important sense underlie these more manifest phenomena. The epistemological canon regarding the treatment of these more theoretical phenomena may be far more akin to that governing any other theoretical posits. So we may find that an information-processing psychology must have a Janus-like character, positing theoretical entities but connecting them to more manifest entities (which it still has an obligation to characterize in a way faithful to their nature in the manifest image).

Chapter 3
The Computational Paradigm: An Overview

This chapter presents an overview of the distinctive methodology of psychology as it is practiced within contemporary cognitive science. Psychology is, of course, a big discipline, and there are at least two senses in which what I have to say will be false of much of it. In the first place, I will discuss only *cognitive* psychology, leaving aside much of developmental psychology, clinical psychology, personality theory, and other specialties within the discipline. This is simply because I am interested in the ontological issues raised by the attempt to understand scientifically the nature of such states as beliefs and the other propositional attitudes, and cognitive psychology is the relevant specialty. Second, among cognitive psychologists there is a diversity of methodologies and ideologies about the discipline. I will ignore that diversity in favor of a characterization that is generally true of most of those psychologists who would also call themselves cognitive scientists. There is a further sense in which my characterization may not ring altogether true to the ears of a cognitive psychologist: It is philosophically motivated, cast in a vocabulary largely alien to psychology, and tuned for a set of issues that are philosophical rather than psychological. Any appearance of infidelity here is a result of this difference in perspective.

I will begin, then, with a characterization of what I call *IPS explanation*—the explanation of a thing's capacities achieved by characterizing it as an information-processing system. In will then characterize the functionalist account of psychological phenomena that this view induces, and conclude with a few brief remarks about how one interprets a functionalist IPS account of human psychological capacities.

It is by now a truism that the digital computer is largely responsible for providing cognitive psychology with a model of explanation (see Haugeland 1981b, 1978; Pylyshyn 1984; Cummins 1983). Computer science demonstrated that, and how, it is possible to explain the apparently intelligent behavior of a complex system without presupposing the intelligence of its components. The essential idea is that of an information-processing system, and this idea brings in tow the computational model of explanation. This model holds out the hope not only of explaining the intelligent by decomposing it into the stupid, but of analyzing intentionality in terms of *functionally interpreted* states of physical systems (what Newell and Simon [1976] have called the idea of a physical symbol system) as well. Finally, this model of mind and explanation suggests a model of the mind-body relation that is respectably physicalistic, in that it does not posit a dualism of substance, but that does not necessarily, or at least does not straight-forwardly, involve the reduction of the mental to the physical.

Imagine how we explain the complex abilities of a suitably programmed computer. We posit subprocesses to explain the actions of processes, sub-subprocesses to explain the actions of subprocesses, and so on, until we get down to the level of elementary information processes. Elementary information processes are easy to explain. They are wired into the central processing unit. Explaining the system's ability to perform them is a matter of detailing its electronics. While the action of a whole program (say, one that proves the four-color theorem) may appear to require brilliance, the processes it decomposes into at the first level (the "main" subroutines) require only moderate brightness. As we go down through the levels of decomposition in the explanation, the spark of intelligence required for the processes at each level gradually dims, until we reach the (electronic equivalents of) flip-flops, which are as dumb as any machine. The ghost is exorcized by gradually reducing it to idiotic nothingness as we elaborate the explanation.

This kind of explanation has been called by Haugeland (1978) *systematic explanation*. The explanandum of a systematic explanation is always a capacity, as opposed to an event or a regularity (the typical explananda of deductive-nomological explanations). The capacity is explained systematically if the thing whose capacity it is is analyzed as a set of interacting components whose individual capacities and interactions together give rise to the capacity being explained. It is of the essence of a systematic explanation (as opposed to a morphological explanation; see Haugeland 1978) that the interactions of the components play an explanatory role. An example of Haugeland's makes this point nicely:

> Now consider a case that is subtly but importantly different [from that of the (morphological) explanation of how a fiber-optics bundle works]: an explanation of how an automobile engine works. As with morphological explanations, this one appeals to a specified structure, and to specified abilities and dispositions of what is so structured. But in addition, and so important as to dominate the account, it requires specification of a complexly organized pattern of interdependent interactions. The various parts of an engine do many different things, so to speak "working together" or "cooperating" in an organized way,

to produce an effect quite unlike what any of them could do alone. (Haugeland 1978 [p. 247 in Haugeland 1981])

Explanations may be systematic "one level down," say, and become morphological or deductive-nomological at lower levels, as the capacities or regularities of the interacting components into which the original system is decomposed by the original explanation are themselves explained. Or, as is typically the case in actual explanations in computer science or psychology, the explanations may look systematic for many levels, as systematic explanations of the capacities of a global system reveal it to be composed of a number of interacting subsystems each of whose capacities are themselves best explained systematically, and so forth.

In any physically instantiated system, such as a human being or a computer, these successive systematic reductions will eventually "bottom out" at a level where the components' capacities or regularities are best explained morphologically or deductive-nomologically. But this level may be utterly uninteresting from the standpoint of capturing generalizations at higher levels of analysis. This point can be made by noting that, for instance, at the level of analysis where the explanations become nonsystematic, the explanations of how an automobile engine made of steel and an otherwise identical one made of high-temperature plastic (were such a thing possible) would look very different, whereas from the standpoint of one asking "How does this engine work?" the explanations in each case would be the same.

A feature of information-processing systems that is a consequence of their systematicity is their *modularity on functional dimensions*. This is a point about what kinds of parts these systems decompose into. Compare three objects: an anvil, an automobile engine, and a story-understanding computer. In order to understand the "behavior" of the anvil under various stresses or weather conditions, we can simply decompose it into a set of adjacent regions and investigate their behavior. But suppose that we tried to explain how an automobile engine works by dividing it exhaustively into a set of adjacent one-inch cubes and then explaining the behavior of each cube and their interactions. One cube might include part of a piston, part of an intake valve, some empty space, and a bit of the wall of a cylinder; another might include a piece of carburetor, some air filter, and part of a wing nut. Many cubes would be largely empty.

It would be much better to decompose the engine into its "natural" modules (the fuel system, the electrical system, the ignition system, the exhaust system, and so on), to explain the behavior of each of these systems (perhaps by decomposing *them* into their natural components), and then to characterize the interactions between these systems. The interesting thing about this strategy (the only one with a hope of providing an explanation) is that the components into which it divides the engine will in general be not spatially individuated but rather *functionally* individuated. The subcomponents of any component subserve the same or related functions, and these functions are hierarchically arranged: The fuel system delivers fuel to the cylinders, the carburetor (a component of the fuel system) mixes the fuel with air, the needle-valve assembly controls the amount of fuel admitted to the carburetor, and so on.

This kind of functional organization is characteristic of information-processing systems as well. However, in information-processing systems, unlike automobile engines, the parts of the system, their functions, and the ways in which they are interconnected are typically characterized *intentionally*—that is, by reference to their representational properties. For instance, a chess-playing computer (when considered as an information-processing system rather than as, say, as an expensive paperweight) would decompose not into adjacent one-inch cubes, nor into components best characterized electronically, but rather into such things as a position decoder, a move generator, a look-ahead device, a tree-pruning routine, and position-evaluation routines. Each of these components is characterized functionally rather than physically. Indeed—and this is an essential feature of information-processing systems—it doesn't matter what physical stuff the components are made of, just so they turn out the right output for each input.

Moreover, each *function*, and hence each device, is characterized intentionally. (Up to this point, we have been using such terms as "intentional" and "intentionality" rather loosely. More careful conceptual refinement is not necessary at this stage, but it will become important in chapter 7.) And this gives us the essence of an information-processing system—a system of representations and representation manipulators that decomposes functionally and whose functions and components are characterized intentionally. (Haugeland [1978] offers a slightly different characterization. His differs from mine primarily in that he requires that an information-processing system be *digital* in a fairly strong sense. This has certain advantages—e.g., in clarifying the connection between current digital technology and cognitive psychology, and perhaps in interpreting much of current psycholinguistic theory in a more straightforward way—but I think that it is too restrictive and that it ignores much that is of interest in contemporary cognitive psychology, particularly in the areas of vision and perhaps mental imagery, where analog models are taken quite seriously. [See, e.g., Block 1981.]) Cognitive science is the attempt to understand the mind as just such a system.

Thus, an information-processing system is a system that represents and encodes information in either a digital or an analog form. (There are a number of versions of the analog/digital distinction, and the precise way in

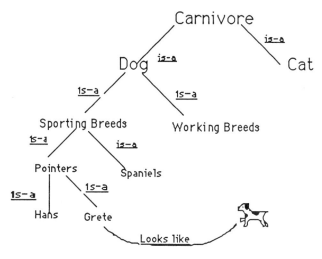

Figure 3.1

which the distinction is drawn is unimportant for present purposes. See Haugeland 1982 or Lewis 1975 for more detailed discussion of this issue.) If it is to operate digitally, using such perfectly precise, error-free (and hence information-preserving) operations as arithmetic, linguistic, and logical operations, the information must be encoded digitally and must presumably be acquired and utilized via transducers mediating between the analog world in which most intelligent organisms live and the digital components of those organisms' information-processing systems. If the system is to operate analogically, exploiting the speed and the fine-grainedness of such analog processes as rotation, expansion, or continuous amplification, the representations it employs must be analogical.

Besides systematicity, as we just noted, the other central feature of an IPS is its intentionality. Just what it takes for a system or a state of a system to be intentional and just what it is to represent one thing rather than another are difficult matters. It seems, at least, necessary that there be an isomorphism between the representational components of the system and the contents of those representations and processes (though it is certainly not necessary for any representational component of such a system itself to *resemble*, in any sense, its content). We would want there to be some sort of structure-preserving mapping between the components of the system that do the representing and the things in the world (or out of it) that they represent. So, if all pointers are sporting dogs, and all sporting dogs are carnivorous, then for me (or a computer database) to represent this set of relations, some structure such as that illustrated in figure 3.1 should be present.

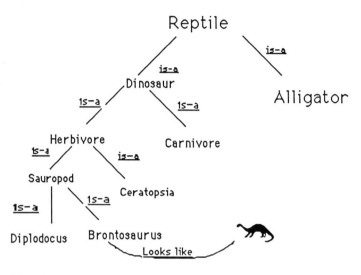

Figure 3.2

Figure 3.1 is an example of a semantic net, a knowledge-representation structure familiar in cognitive science. The real information, of course, is carried not by the nodes but rather by the links (not to mention the interpretive processes and structures responsible for representing and utilizing the net). Presumably the reason that this net can represent the information it does is that the relations between the nodes in the net mirror the relations between the corresponding entities and classes in the world. (Of course there is a vast difference between this isomorphism of structure and the isomorphism between Grete's image and Grete that enables the image to represent her. Whether there can be such analog representations in a human or an artificial system is a hotly debated matter; see Block 1980a, Block 1981, and Pylyshyn 1984. In the case of imagistic representation, (if it ever occurs), a great deal of the information is carried by the image, and not all the information is carried by its relation to other nodes.)

But we can show easily that this relation of isomorphism is not sufficient to make the net *about* these dogs and related matters. Consider figure 3.2. This net is isomorphic to that represented in figure 3.1. But even though they are each about something, they are not about the same things. What would capture this difference? One answer is that the ways in which these nets hook up with perception and action would differ. The "dog net," for instance, might somehow be involved with throwing sticks for Grete, and the "dinosaur net" might be similarly involved with strolling through the dinosaur exhibit of a museum. (For a possible account of this relation between such nets and their referents in terms of selective activation of nodes in response to new information or goals, see Anderson 1976 and 1983.) The point is that intentionality requires not only isomorphism but also some kind of appropriate relation (perhaps input-output relations) to the world. Not only must the representational structures in the mind or machine be isomorphic to what they represent; since, as our two examples show, any mental structure will be isomorphic to a host of different things (and vice versa), a representational structure, in order to represent some state of affairs, must be associated in some richer way (in some cases a causal connection, in others a more indirect connection via linguistic or other conventions) with that state of affairs, or something like it, and must be connected in some way with behavior appropriate to that state of affairs, or something like it. To tell this story in any further detail would be unnecessary for present purposes as well as extraordinarily difficult (perhaps impossible), and would take us far beyond the purview of this study.

On this account, of course, computing systems count as intentional systems. Some, including Searle (1980), balk at this suggestion. Others, like Baker (1987), distinguish between *original* and *derived* intentionality. They ascribe the former to humans and perhaps other animals in virtue of something like the "naturalness" of our mental states' relations to their contents, and the latter to the artificial systems, including machines and natural languages. These derivedly intentional systems, according to the proponents of this distinction, are intentional only because we, in virtue of interpreting them, ascribe them content. In chapter 7 I will distinguish two grades of intentionality. However, this distinction will in no way coincide with the putative distinction just adumbrated. The distinction between original and derived intentionality is a red herring. *All* intentionality is a matter of relations actually obtaining between representations and their contents. The provenance of these relations is beside the point for understanding their nature. (Presumably, if computers grew, suitably programmed and ready to go, on trees, their intentionality would be of a piece with that of conventional artificial-intelligence systems; and if people could be brewed, in adult form, by sophisticated chemical engineers, theirs would be of a piece with ours.) This, however, is a side issue (with roots in Sellars and Chisholm 1972).

These two features of an information-processing system may not be sufficient for it to be intentional. Many, including Searle (1980, 1983), argue that more is necessary; we will return to this issue in more detail in chapter 7. However, these two features at least seem clearly necessary, and seem at least to be central features of the representational power of human and artificial representational information-processing systems.

On the above model, our cognitive states—our beliefs, desires, moods, hopes, and fears—are states of our information-processing system. Now, exactly what this means is a matter of some dispute, but the rough idea is that, just as a computer's moving its pawn to King's four is, when carefully examined, just an informational characterization of a particular physical state of that computer (voltage high on such and such a line, etc.), my moving my pawn to King's four is just a way of informationally characterizing *my* physical state (including, perhaps, the movement of my arm and the current pattern of neural firings). Cognitive psychology attempts to elucidate the nature of the information processes that mediate between our neural wetware and our beliefs and other conscious states.

Understanding the IPS approach makes it clear just why our pretheoretic intuitions about the domain of psychology may turn out to be in need of drastic revision. Pretheoretically it might seem strange to lump psychology (possibly a branch of neuroscience, seemingly about humans) with artificial intelligence (a branch of computer science, seemingly about machines). But if the mind is understood as an IPS, an abstractly characterized formal structure for manipulating representations, then it would seem that the relevant theoretical domain for the study of cognition is not that of brain-stuff *per se* but rather that of the IPS, a domain in which humans and machines may be compatriots.

In this section I want to arrive at a reasonable characterization of the model of the psychophysical relation suggested by the IPS model of the mind. It is generally called functionalism, but that label covers a wide variety of metaphysical positions. I want to end up with a characterization of a functionalism that is a fair description of what cognitive science is committed to in adopting the IPS model and that is also general enough so that it does not characterize only a corner of the field. In the final section of this chapter, we will turn to the question of how to *interpret* information-processing theories of human intelligence: Are psychological processes really carried out by the brain in some kind of biological analog of LISP code, or are the programs written by psychologists and computer scientists engaged in cognitive simulation merely useful calculational devices for predicting human behavior? This will complete the preliminary stage-setting for a discussion of the place of the propositional attitudes in psychology.

The most primitive version of functionalism is *machine functionalism.* Machine functionalism takes as its model of the mind the Turing machine, noting that it is a physical system and at the same time an abstract calculational device. Whenever a Turing machine is in a particular physical state, it is also in a particular machine state, and it is performing some particular calculation—say, adding two numbers—or emulating some other Turing machine. And there is no great mystery, no "mind-body problem," about how the *physical* machine manages to be at the same time a *computing* machine—about how its machine or computational states are related to its physical states. If someone were to ask how this merely physical machine could possibly be performing the "mental operation" of adding, we would simply point out that each machine state of the system just is a physical state of the system under a computational description.

Machine functionalism asserts that it might be just the same with us humans. After all, Turing machines can represent any information-processing system we instantiate. They, and we, are finite (though unbounded) physical systems. Hence, if we are physically instantiated information-processing systems, as cognitive science would have it, we are functionally equivalent to some Turing machine. Since, for a Turing machine, to be in a particular machine state (its analog of a psychological state) is to be in a particular functionally interpreted physical state, it is overwhelmingly plausible to assert that, for humans, to be in a particular psychological state is to be in a particular functionally interpreted physical state (presumably a biological state of the central nervous system.) After all, this line of reasoning continues, a Turing machine can be realized in any kind of physical medium, including both metal and neural matter. So it would seem that human neural states are to be thought of first as machine states and then as psychological states. The task of cognitive science, on this view, is to uncover the machine table that characterizes the machines that are instantiated by people. (For the classic exposition of this view, see Putnam 1960.)

This primitive machine functionalism, however, proves to be too restrictive. One essential feature of a Turing machine is its fixed, unchanging, finite list of machine states. But even though the number of machine states for any Turing machine is finite, the number of possible computations that a machine can perform is, in general, infinite. Consider a Turing machine A, which is just an adder. Now, though A may have a very simple machine table, involving only a few states, if we characterize A not by reference to its machine states but by reference to what we might call instead its computational states, we will see that there are an indefinite number of states in which A is capable of being. It might be adding 2 and 3, or adding 666,666 and 994, or "carrying 2," or "writing the answer." Though each of these computational states is equivalent to some *sequence* of machine states and tape sequences, none is identifiable with any single machine state, and, in virtue of the unboundedness of the set of possible sequences of machine states, there are infinitely many possible computational states of A.

The view that human psychological states are to humans as computational states are to Turing machines is *psychofunctionalism*. Two general sorts of grounds motivate psychofunctionalism as opposed to machine functionalism. The first kind has to do with the apparent unboundedness of the class of human psychological states with which we would like our theories to cope; the second kind has to do with the criteria we would adduce for the ascription of psychological states to humans or machines. Let us consider these in turn.

Suppose that humans are, in an appropriate sense, equivalent to some Turing machines. Then we have finitely many possible machine states. But it appears that, for instance, we are capable of an indefinite number of possible beliefs. We can, for instance, believe that 2 is the successor of 1, that 3 is the successor of 2, and so on, for all pairs of natural numbers. Considerations such as this motivate the view that the number of possible psychological states that a complete cognitive science must account for vastly outstrips the number of machine states possible for any Turing machine, although, as we have seen, any Turing machine of even small complexity is capable of infinitely many computational states.

This argument does not rely on the premise that the brain is capable of assuming infinitely many neurobiologically discriminably distinct physical states (a premise that may be false if the "grain" of neurophysiological ontology is substantially coarser than that of the underlying biophysics, which is more or less continuous). It might well be (and I will argue in chapters 5 and 7 that this is indeed the case) that the indefinite number of possible psychological states issues, rather, from the facts that the identity conditions for psychological states are relational, and that there are an indefinite number of psychologically interesting relations that persons can bear to their environment. But just as we get a richer description of any finite Turing machine by talking about its computational states than by talking about its machine states (both in that there are many more of the former than the latter and in that the former are in general far more interesting to us than the latter), we would get a much richer (and hence, perhaps, psychologically more fertile) description of our brains by talking about their computational states than by talking about their machine states.

Even if one believed that there are only finitely many psychological states in which we are capable of being, there are reasons to prefer in some circumstances the psychofunctional account of psychological states. Suppose I have two Turing machines, T^1 and T^2. Both are adding machines, and both are made of the same material. But suppose that their machine tables and sets of machine states are different in the following way: Where T^1 adds by successively incrementing the first addend by 1 the number of times specified by the second addend, T^2 adds by incrementing the second addend by 1 the number of times specified by the first addend, and does this using a different set of machine states. Now, it seems fair to say that when these two machines are adding a pair of numbers, they are, in an important sense, doing the same thing. If we count them as "believing" anything about the sums they compute, then they "agree" in all their "beliefs," despite the fact that they share no machine states. Hence, it seems that the computational level of description is, for some purposes at least, a useful one for the description of Turing machines.

The case for people seems, if anything, clearer. Whereas it seems tenuous to attribute beliefs to adding machines, and odd to think that the computational level would be a particularly interesting level of description for them, it is at least plausible that among the psychologically interesting facts about people are the things they believe, fear, and doubt. And even if we are, underneath our surface psychology, Turing machines, many different Turing machines could realize these surface states. Further, even on a strongly functionalist account of psychological states, it seems that our criteria for attributing these states to ourselves and to others have nothing whatever to do with our views about the machine tables underlying our cognitive processes but rather have to do with the relations that these states stand in to other such states, to the inputs we receive from our environments, and to the behavior we produce in response to them. For instance, if I am disposed to say "Goats are wonderful," to argue vigorously with those who doubt the virtues of goats, to act in an admiring and friendly way toward goats, to infer from the fact that goats are nearby that something wonderful is nearby, and so on, you can quite comfortably ascribe to me the belief that goats are wonderful. And this belief, though it may be supported by some set of my machine states, tape states, and so on, needn't be identified with any particular machine state. And it certainly needn't be the case that there is some machine state such that anyone who shares my belief is in *that state*. Psychofunctionalism hence appears to be a more plausible and a somewhat higher-level version of functionalism than machine functionalism. (See Fodor and Block 1972 and Block 1980a for excellent discussions of the varieties and the problems of functionalism.)

As liberal as psychofunctionalism appears in its account of the psychophysical relation, it is possible to develop a still less restrictive account that is still recognizably functionalist. In order to understand what I will call *representational functionalism*, it is necessary to step back from the machine metaphor and to consider what it is that makes an account functionalist in the first place. Both machine functionalism and psychofunctionalism develop the general idea of functionalism using the Turing machine as the leading idea. But that is really not an essential feature of the functionalist approach. The kernel of the approach is really the insight that psychological terms such as "belief", "desire", "pain", "memory", and "perception" need not be understood as some kind of shorthand either for neurophysiological descriptions or for behavioral descriptions.

The view that psychological descriptions are shorthand for neurophysiological descriptions is, of course, the old *central state identity theory*. (See Smart 1959 and Armstrong 1968 for classic expositions of this view, and Fodor 1981 and Lewis 1980 for criticisms.) An unfortunate consequence of this view is that only beings who are neurophysiologically like humans can have psychological states (or at least psychological states like ours). That rules out in a single *a priori* stroke the possibility of intelligent (or even sentient) Martians or computers. In fact, it rules out the possibility of many humans' sharing any states as well: Consider two twin brothers, Sinister and Dexter. When the boys were under one year old, they were involved in a terrible automobile accident. Sinister lost the left half of his brain; Dexter lost his right half. Fortunately, both were young enough that they have completely recovered with no loss of function, and both believe that snow is white. If the central state identity theory were true, we would be forced to say that, despite their apparently similar belief, they in fact share no psychological properties.

Thinking that our psychological vocabulary is a set of shorthands for behavioral descriptions is, of course, behaviorism. On this view, to ascribe to both Mary and Sue the desire for a pet unicorn would be to assert that they share a batch of *behavioral dispositions*, including such things as the tendency to chase and attempt to capture any passing unicorns, to say things like "Boy, I wish I had a pet unicorn," to search the "Pet Store" section of the Yellow Pages tirelessly for a store carrying unicorns, and so forth. But suppose that Mary is painfully diffident and hence never says anything demanding, and has never heard of the Yellow Pages, while Sue is a brash and cosmopolitan New Yorker. Then, on a behaviorist account, they could not share this (or for that matter, probably any) desire, since their dispositions are radically different.

The Scylla of central state identity theory has this much going for it: It lets Mary and Sue share a desire, despite their personality differences, and gives us a fairly straightforward answer to any question about the nature of the psychophysical relation. Unfortunately, it delivers the wrong answer on Dexter and Sinister, and it loses us the Martians and the computers altogether. The Charybdis of behaviorism has this much going for it: It lets Bill and John, despite their very different neurophysiological makeup, share a memory, in virtue of their being disposed to say and do the same relevant things, and it preserves our intuitions about the Martians. But it gets Mary and Sue wrong, and more besides (beyond the scope of this discussion, but see, e.g., Lewis 1980).

Functionalism navigates the narrow strait by giving each side its due. The functionalist agrees with the behaviorist that the connections between psychological states and the organism's input and output are central to that state's nature, and that psychological states are independent of particular physical realizations in particular organisms or machines. But the functionalist also agrees with the identity theorist that it is important to look at the *inside* of the organism, and the interrelations of *internal* states, in assigning psychological predicates to physical correlates. The functionalist differs from both in suggesting that the right way to understand the mind-body relation is via a *token-identity theory*; that is, to assert that particular (token) psychological events are to be identified with token physical events. Both the behaviorist and the identity theorist subscribe to the stronger *type-identity* theory, whereon each type (that is, each kind) of psychological event is to be identified with a type of physical (for the identity theorist) or behavioral (for the behaviorist) event. The greater flexibility of this token-identity position provides the compass that guides the passage.

What emerges from this picture of the general position staked out by functionalism is that, while the Turing-machine-inspired models of machine functionalism and psychofunctionalism are versions of this view, they are not the only possible versions. In order for a theory to count as functionalist, it is necessary only that it claim that token psychological states are to be identified with token physical states under *some* scheme for identification, so long as that scheme identifies the psychological states in a vocabulary by making essential reference to their role in the psychology of their bearers, where that role is characterized by reference to their relations to other such states, to processes operating over them, and to functionally characterized inputs and outputs. It is not necessary, in order to count as functionalist, for a theory to be committed to any particular scheme.

The representational functionalist (Pylyshyn [1984] and Lycan [1981] are two notable champions of this view) will agree that whatever the scheme is, it must pay attention to the functional role that the psychological state in question plays in the system being studied—that is, to its relations to inputs, outputs, and other internal states. What distinguishes the representational functionalist from the psychofunctionalist is the interpolation of a level of description between the level at which such psychological phenomena as PAs, qualia, and the other commonsense phenomena are to be found (call it, following Pylyshyn [1984], the *representational level*) and the level at which the token physical states with which these are ultimately to be identified are found (the *physical level*). Pylyshyn (1984) calls this the *functional level*. (See also Haugeland [1978] on intentional instantiation and interpretation.)

We can now sketch an intuitive picture of the distinctions between explaining the behavior of a complex, intelligent organism at the physical, functional, and representational levels, in order to get clearer. Suppose a system is writing a commentary on *Moby Dick*. First, if you could explain the system's behavior at the physical level, it would give you an accuracy of predictive power unmatched by either of the other strategies. You could even predict (and this you could not do even in principle in the other strategies) when the organism would drop from exhaustion. The problems, of course, are that such an explanation is, in practice, impossible, and that, although it tells you how this organism really works in one sense, it fails utterly to tell you how it thinks about literature. Consider another system, this one a machine that is functionally identical to our hypothetical organism but is made of silicon chips. Any explanation of how our organism criticizes literature should be an explanation of how the machine does so, since they run exactly the same program; however, the physical explanation of the behavior of our computer will be entirely irrelevant, and certainly wildly false of its organic twin. Hence, whatever the physical explanation does explain, it doesn't explain our machine's or our organism's critical ability *per se*.

Explanation at the functional level avoids this problem, since it would assign the same explanation to our two physically dissimilar but computationally equivalent critics. It would also be easier to come up with. These are its principal advantages. On the other hand, the functional approach suffers a few drawbacks of its own: First, though it is easier to come up with a functional explanation of the abilities of such a system than it is to come up with the corresponding physical explanation, it is still terribly difficult, and the explanation might be so complex that it would provide no real insight into the ability at all. Secondly, and unavoidably, there is much that the functional explanation will be absolutely unable to handle, such as malfunctions of the machine or diseases of the organism which are perfectly amenable to physical explanation but which are simply beyond the purview of the functional standpoint. Finally, there is a problem facing the functional approach that is analogous to the problem of rigidity we saw plaguing the physical approach, though it emerges at a slightly higher level. Consider two chess-playing machines, alike in hardware, running programs that implement the same general chess-playing strategies, using the same chess algorithms and heuristics, but are written in different programming languages, using different types of underlying machine language subroutines, data structures, and control. Ideally, we would want an explanation of how they play chess to be the same for both. But that would require a "higher," more abstract level of description than the programming strategy. A similar possibility can be envisioned for our critics.

That more abstract level, of course, is what Pylyshyn (1984) has called the representational level. Here, instead of talking about transistors or neurons, or about subroutines or short-term memory stacks, we talk about plans, goals, desires, beliefs, knowledge, and the rest. The disadvantages of this strategy in comparison with the first two are plain: Its predictions will be far less exact, and its explanations in particular cases will be that much more suspect. It will be completely unable to handle hardware malfunctions and software "bugs." But its advantages are impressive as well. A reasonable amount of close observation will yield pretty good theories at this level, and the theories will be relatively easy to test and to implement for prediction. Most of all, explanations at this mentalistic level will generalize to all machines and organisms performing the same kinds of criticism in the same way. Hence, they will really provide an explanation of *how they criticize literature*, in a way appropriate to explaining *literary criticism*.

The idea is this: There are generalizations about humans that are best captured at the physiological level of description, including, no doubt, neurophysiological generalizations of interest to psychology. There are also generalizations of interest that cannot be captured at the physiological level but rather must be captured at a functional level of description, simply because there may be only a token-identity relation and no type-identity relation obtaining between the physiological states underlying the functionally characterized states of an organism and those functionally characterized states themselves, as in the case of Bill and John or, more radically, in the case of a human and a silicon-based Martian with a virtually identical psychology. So, like the psychofunctionalist, the representational functionalist anticipates a multitude of possible physical architectures underlying a single functional architecture. Where the representational functionalist parts company is in applying the same argument to the relation between the functional level and the representational or symbol level.

Just as we can imagine physically dissimilar objects being truthfully characterized by the same psychological generalizations, in virtue of the fact that those generalizations obtain at the functional rather than the physical level of description, we can imagine beings with very different functional architectures but with similar representational states. Suppose, for instance, that (contrary to fact) humans add small numbers by installing a representation of each in short-term memory along with a lookup table of all small sums and then computing the result by matching the addends to the appropriate line in the lookup table, whereas Martians, behaviorally indistinguishable from us, do it by installing both addends and then successively incrementing the first addend by one, while reducing the second addend by one, until the second equals zero. It might be that only very sensitive reaction-time experiments can detect this difference. Now, it might be that our psychology differs from the Martians' in countless such ways (each invisible to the unaided eye), despite our sharing most commonsense, representational properties, including beliefs, capacities, and inferential tendencies. In such a case it would be reasonable to say that, while we are functionally very different, we are symbolically, or representationally, roughly equivalent. That is, in such a case, all generalizations at the representational level true of us would be true of them, while none of the generalizations true of us at the functional level would be true of them.

The vocabulary that is appropriate, on this account, to the description of psychological organisms or machines at the representational level is that vocabulary in terms of which semantic or representational generalizations can be stated, or semantic or representational theories constructed (that is, the vocabulary of intentional idioms where the contents of intentional constructions can be, among other things, objects in the external world). The vocabulary appropriate to the functional level, by contrast, is that of a computational theory of the organism, where the phenomena posited, while they are interpreted (as they must be, given that they are nonphysical), are interpreted merely as computational states.

Now, there is at least one important respect in which the sketches I have offered of these levels of description are oversimplified. I have talked all along as though there is a unique, easily characterized functional level of description of any complex information-processing system, a unique, easily characterized representational level, and a unique, easily characterized physical level. In fact, for any interestingly complex system, there are numerous such levels, and the distinctions between them are often hard to draw and matter-of-degreeish (see Lycan [unpublished]). Explanations of many interesting phenomena may require mention of processes identified at one or more of each of the physical, functional, and representational levels appropriate to the description of a given system. Consider, for example, Marr's (1982) theory of vision, which explains human object perception using a mixture of levels of description and in which explanations at each of these levels are essential, or Arbib's (1987) similar discussion of visuomotor coordination in frogs and toads, where both computational and neurophysiological explanations play essential roles. This oversimplification is a useful expository device, however, and I believe it does not impugn the points I am after regarding the characterization of functionalism or cognitivism.

Before we leave the topic of the varieties of functionalism, it is necessary to settle on a version that most accurately characterizes the view of the mind embodied by current work in cognitive psychology. I will do that rather quickly, despite the fact that there is considerable room for debate. Machine functionalism is a nonstarter. It is by now a historical curiosity, and useful only as a device for introducing the more sophisticated versions of functionalism that now dominate the scene. Psychofunctionalism is a philosopher's doctrine. It "flattens" the complexity of the relation between representation and physiology in a way that is useful for making certain important points about the ontological distinctness of these levels of description, despite the dependency of the higher level upon the more fundamental; however, the simplification it introduces is not true to the flavor of current psychological theory. Only representational functionalism, with its greater flexibility and its greater sensitivity to the multitude of theoretical layers that may need to be interpolated in cognitive theory between neurons and beliefs, is seriously held by practitioners of cognitive science, and it is the only functionalist theory of the mind-body relation that can truly said to be embodied by that program. Henceforth, when I refer to functionalism, it will be representational functionalism that I have in mind.

It is a metaphilosophical fact that even those who are tough-minded scientific realists about physical or biological theory suddenly may become instrumentalists when confronted with psychological theories. (I leave aside those who simply believe that psychology is impossible, or that all current psychology is irredeemably false.) Not wanting to replay the instrumentalist-realist debate in general terms here, I refer the interested reader to Van Fraassen 1980 or to Churchland 1979. Rather, I propose to assume that a realistic interpretation of scientific theories makes sense for physical science, and to ask whether there might be special problems for the realistic interpretation of psychological theory. The question is crucial, because if one could argue that—despite the reality of the objects in the ontologies of physical theories, and despite the presence in the ontology of psychology of such phenomena as PAs and qualia—psychological theory deserves a merely instrumentalistic interpretation, then one could argue that psychological phenomena need not be taken seriously as real. There are three principal arguments for psychological instrumentalism (recalling our assumption that a realistic interpretation is appropriate for physical theory). I will call them the *argument from fiction*, the *argument from interpretation*, and the *argument from the unity of science*, and I will consider each in turn, arguing that none of them is compelling.

The *locus classicus* for the argument from fiction is Dennett 1982. (See chapters 1, 5, and 7 of Dennett 1978 for earlier versions, and Cummins 1983 for a slightly different version, directed more toward intentional ascriptions *per se*.) Dennett argues that the psychological phenomena that are to be found at the representational level are best construed as *notional* attitudes, or attitudes toward objects in the subjects' notional world:

> A notional world should be seen as a sort of *fictional* world devised by a theorist, a third-party observer, in order to characterize the narrow-psychological states of a subject. A notional world can be supposed to be full of notional objects, and the scene of notional events—all the objects and events the subject *believes in*, you might say....
>
> The idea of a notional world, then, is the idea of a model—but not necessarily the actual, real, true model—of one's internal representations. *It does not consist itself of representations but of representeds....* The theorist wishing to characterize the narrow-psychological states of a creature, or in other words, the organismic contribution of that creature to its propositional attitudes, *describes* a fictional world.... (1982, pp. 38, 40)

On this view, which is an elaboration of the view sketched in chapter 1 of Dennett 1978, representational states consist in notional attitudes in an environmental context. The notional attitude attribution is the theorist's description of the organism's internal state; the propositional attitude attribution is the composition of the notional attitude and the theorist's characterization of the environmental context in which the organism and its notional attitude are situated.

But the element of fiction and the contribution of the theorist are taken very seriously by this account. The psychological phenomena that appear at the representational level on this account appear only because theorists (including auto-theorists) find it predictively and explanatorily convenient to posit them. And just as their objects are typically fictional, the intentional phenomena themselves are ultimately "theorists' fictions." What is actually going on in the organism is what is described at the physical or, at most, the functional level. The only reason that we don't describe and explain the organism's behavior and capacities at these more fundamental levels is that we are ignorant of its structure at these levels. (See also Dennett 1971.) So we do the best we can: We imagine an environment for which it is suited and ascribe to it states appropriate to that environment, counting ourselves successful when we achieve a reasonable degree of predictive success. None of this theoretical activity, however, presupposes any commitment to the reality of the attitudes we ascribe to the organism, any more than it presupposes the reality of the organism's notional world, toward which these attitudes are directed. Indeed, to commit ourselves ontologically to these phenomena would be, on this account, a fallacious inference from the heuristic value of what we know to be our fictional creation to the reality of the elements contained therein.

Dennett is even more explicit about the instrumentalism embodied in this view in his 1971 essay:

> ... Skinner is right in recognizing that intentionality can be no *foundation* for psychology, and right also in looking for purely mechanistic regularities in the activities of his subjects.... In seeking knowledge of internal design our most promising tactic is to take out intelligence-loans, endow peripheral and internal events with content, and then look for mechanisms that will function appropriately with such "messages" so that we can pay back the loans. (Dennett 1971; in Dennett 1978a, p. 17)
>
> ... If one wants to get away from norms and predict and explain the "actual, empirical" behavior ... one stops talking of their *chess moves* and starts talking of their proclivities to move pieces of wood or ivory about on checkered boards; if one wants to predict and explain the "actual, empirical" behavior of believers, one must similarly cease

talking of belief, and descend to the design stance or physical stance for one's account. (ibid., p. 22)

What motivates this instrumentalistic attitude toward representations is, at bottom, a Quinean thesis about the indeterminacy of translation and about the translational/interpretive nature of attitude ascription. The image of attitude ascription here is that of coming across a presumably intelligent alien and attempting to translate what one presumes is its speech. In such a case, we are simultaneously attempting to vindicate the accuracy of a translation manual and the accuracy of an ascription of a conceptual scheme to the alien. The inability to know anything about the one without prior confidence in the other renders any translation that gets the alien believing mostly the truth, desiring mostly the desirable, and acting for the most part rationally as good as any other translation that gets him equally sane. But, of course, there are an infinite number of mutually inconsistent translation schemes that will accomplish this, and, the story goes, we can have no reason to prefer any one over any other. So all such radical translation is indeterminate.

Now, if one accepts the thesis of the indeterminacy of translation, and the thesis that representation ascription is an instance of translation, and the thesis that any *real* states of an organism (that is, states to which a realistically interpreted psychological theory is ontologically committed) are *determinate* (each have a uniquely justifiable theoretical characterization), it follows that representational states are not real in this sense—that the assignment of any representational state to an organism cannot preclude the assignment of indefinitely many other incompatible states to that organism—and hence that the only criterion of accuracy for such ascriptions can be one of utility and not one of truth. And to give up on any assertion of the truth of the existence claims in one's theory is to treat its posits as fictional. This is the essence of the argument from fiction, which at bottom is an argument from indeterminacy.

But the argument should not compel us. There are three considerations that cast doubt upon the soundness of this argument for the special instrumentality of representational ascriptions, one of which casts doubts on each of the three premises. In the first place, the argument assumes that there is a special determinateness and hence a special reality to the phenomena posited by the physical sciences—that while the ascriptions of representational properties by psychological claims can at best pick out one of a number of equally good hypotheses concerning the actual state of the system or organism at issue, in virtue of the indeterminacy of translation, ascriptions of physical properties to systems or organisms can be true (can pick out just the state or process that is actually occurring). This assumption neglects the fact that the thesis of the indeterminacy of translation is really a corollary of a more general thesis: that of the underdetermination of theories by data. Just as there are an indefinite number of representational hypotheses about an organism that might be justified on the basis of any particular set of observations of it, there are an indefinite number of equally justified *physical* theories about any such organism given any similar set of observations. There is hence no *special* indeterminacy about the psychological. (See Quine 1960, esp. § 7.)

Things are actually a bit more complex than this. Quine argues (and others dispute; see, e.g., Chomsky 1972) that indeterminacy cuts much deeper than underdetermination. While underdetermination ceases to obtain when all the data are in, even the totality of a linguistic corpus leaves meaning assignments indeterminate. There are several things to say about this: First, the claim is arguably false. Wartenburg and Ross (1983) argue persuasively that once underdetermination is taken care of, any remaining plethora of equally justified interpretive hypotheses with respect to a total linguistic corpus ought to be treated as notational variants of a single such hypothesis. Second, even if the thesis of special indeterminacy is accepted, it is an epistemological claim with regard to the description of a set of phenomena, and does not straightforwardly entail any ontological claims (more of this below). Third, the indeterminacy thesis posits an indeterminacy in the assignment of meanings (conceived as abstract entities) to linguistic types. My Sellarsian analysis of belief ascription will sidestep this problem by taking the uses of linguistic tokens as primitive. The thesis of special indeterminacy can't get a grip there.

Moreover, this argument assumes (and Quine argues) that all representational ascription is like *radical* translation. The thesis of indeterminacy is far more plausible in the case of radical translation than it is in the case of translation of the utterances of those we know to share at least the greater part of our own conceptual scheme and linguistic conventions. Translation is surer still if we have a pretty good psychological theory in hand to guide us. In fact, if we are ascribing representational states to organisms like us who participate in the same linguistic community we do and whose psychology, as measured by a plausible, well-confirmed theory, is very much like ours, it is tantamount to a necessary condition of intelligent discourse with them, which *ex hypothesi* is occurring, that we can accurately translate their language. Hence, the indeterminacy that permeates this activity, however real, must be negligible. (Again, see Quine 1960.)

Finally, the argument assumes that if there is ineliminable indeterminacy about the correct representational characterization of the state of an organism or a system, the representations posited ought not to be considered real. This claim seems to commit a version of a use/mention confusion: What is indeterminate is the choice of a language in which to characterize the representational state of the system. This indeterminacy need not issue in the unreality of the state being characterized, for there is nothing incoherent about suggesting that there is a perfectly determinate representational state of a system that can be mapped, for the purposes of theoretical description and explanation, onto a large class of descriptions.

I have belabored this argument for psychological instrumentalism at such length because the second argument is very closely related and can now be articulated and dispensed with in much briefer compass. It is the argument from interpretation. Dennett (1978), Cummins (1983), and Searle (1980) flirt with this argument. Suggestions of it are also to be found in Stich 1983. In brief, the argument runs as follows: Representational characterizations are our *interpretations* of the physical (or functional) states of organisms or systems. The phenomena themselves do not "come with" these interpretations as "givens." In themselves they are physical states (which, to be sure, are candidates for interpretation), but they are not *in themselves* interpreted. Hence, the interpretations we assign them are best thought of as our instruments to facilitate their description and explanation, and not as part of reality *per se*—that is, their having the interpretations they do is a function solely of our interpretive activity, and not of any intrinsic property of those states.

The problem with this argument is that it presupposes that physical phenomena, in contrast with psychological phenomena, come with their descriptions in terms of physical theory "on their sleeves." And this is surely false. The task of any science, physical or psychological, is in part to sort out the class of predicates suited to the study of the range of objects in its domain, and the conditions of application of each. The upshot of this enterprise is the discovery of the correct characterization of the objects in the domain of a science, but this is no more true of a science of representations than it is of a science of chemicals. (Lycan [unpublished] argues that functionalism is in fact a true theory not only of mind but of all matter—that every description is a functional description relative to some more fundamental description, and that there is hence nothing special about the functional or representational predicates of psychology in respect of their functionality, or interpretive character.)

The final argument for psychological instrumentalism I will consider is the argument from the unity of science. This argument is advanced most forcefully in Churchland 1979, Churchland 1984, and Churchland and Churchland 1982. It is an argument with a long tradition (as these traditions go) in the philosophy of science, having recognizable ancestors in, for instance, Carnap 1932. In the discussion of theoretical reduction in chapter 2 above, we have already encountered the argument in a slightly different form. It goes like this: The natural world forms a seamless whole, governed by a closed set of deterministic laws. Those laws receive their most fundamental and general formulation in the laws of theoretical physics. The generalizations of all other sciences are, if true, reducible to the laws of physics. Hence, any representational generalization is either false or reducible to physiology and physics. Paul Churchland gives us a number of reasons (which will be considered in detail in chapters 4 and 6 below) to believe that representational generalizations are not reducible to physics. Hence, the only legitimate use of these generalizations could be one that is instrumentalistic in spirit. (Churchland himself denies that even this use is legitimate in science, but we will leave that aside for now.)

This argument is quite different in spirit from the previous two, for it argues not for the instrumental interpretation of a functionalist theory but rather, at bottom, for the abandonment of functionalism in virtue of its falsity on a realistic interpretation. However, it can also be interpreted as a general argument for the instrumentalistic interpretation of any theory that is scientifically useful (if only heuristically) but has not yet been reduced to more fundamental physical sciences, and this is certainly the case with contemporary cognitive science. So interpreted, the argument is not so much unsound as ontologically bigoted. For it would take a powerful argument to convince us that physics, alone among the sciences, is the arbiter of the existent. Even Churchland seems to treat sciences that are far less fundamental than physics, such as chemistry and even neuroscience, with considerable ontological respect. Further, it is far from clear that all true sciences are reducible to a common fundamental science. It is perfectly coherent to assert that the world as described by psychology supervenes on that as described by physics but to deny that, on that account, psychology must be reducible to physics. In a scientific image constituted by a number of compatible but mutually irreducible sciences, there must be room for ontological pluralism, and realistic treatment cannot be apportioned arbitrarily. (See Fodor 1974 and Garfield 1983 for a more fully articulated version of this view.)

I conclude that there is no good reason to treat a cognitive psychology providing explanations at a functional or representational level of description as making weaker ontological claims about its theoretical posits than those made by the physical sciences, and hence that the theories of such a psychology are entitled to a realistic interpretation.

Interpreting representational theories realistically does raise interesting problems about the psychological reality of cognitive theories, which are typically framed (at least implicitly, and often literally) as computer programs. Given that any particular program implements a particular algorithm, is written in a particular programming language, and is compiled to run on a particular virtual machine implemented in a particular kind of hardware, one must be careful in specifying the level of description at which the psychological model proposed by the program is to be interpreted as real. This is not an issue that is central to our investigation, but the interested reader is referred to Pylyshyn 1984, especially chapter 4, for an excellent discussion. Pylyshyn argues persuasively that the algorithm is what should be taken as embodying a psychological theory of the functional states underlying representations. It is, he suggests, the task of cognitive psychology to determine what the functional architecture (the virtual machine) of the mind is, in part through discovering which algorithms it can and does run in the course of realizing its representational phenomena. Choices between functionally equivalent (in the mathematical sense) algorithms are to be made, he suggests, by means of evidence from reaction times, complexity, and other performance-related parameters capable of distinguishing algorithms from one another in real time.

This concludes this overview of the cognitive paradigm. Henceforth, when discussing cognitive psychology, I will be assuming a psychology employing IPS explanation, embodying a representational functionalist theory of mind, and interpreted realistically. Questions about its ontology, and about the place of the commonsense psychological phenomena therein, will be questions about the ontology of such a psychology.

Chapter 4

The Place of the Propositional Attitudes in Psychology: The Problem and the Standard Solutions

With the preliminaries behind us, we are ready for the principal part of this investigation. I will begin by examining the *prima facie* problem posed for cognitive psychology by the propositional attitudes, and will then turn to examples of the four standard approaches to resolving .this problem. In outlining the problem, I will discuss first the standard criteria for a psychological phenomenon counting as a PA, then some conditions imposed on psychological phenomena *per se* by the cognitive paradigm, and finally the nature of the difficulty posed by the apparent clash of these sets of requirements.

Propositional attitudes at least appear to involve relations between persons and propositions. Thus, it would seem that getting an account of the nature of the PAs would require first some account of the nature of propositions, both as they are conceived of by folk psychology and as they are conceived of by contemporary cognitive psychology. Dennett (1982) rehearses Frege's three conditions on propositions, and concludes that, though they motivate all standard accounts of the relation between persons and propositions and of the nature of propositions, they are in fact mutually incompatible. The three desiderata, according to Dennett (1982, pp. 6–7) are these:

> (a) It is a (final, constant, underived) *truth-value bearer*. If *p* is true and *q* false, *p* and *q* are not the same proposition....
> (b) It is composed of *intensions*, where intensions are understood *à la* Carnap as extension-determiners. Different intensions can determine the same extension.... Different extensions cannot be determined by one intension, however.
> (c) It is graspable by the mind.

Propositions, writes Dennett (1982, p. 10),

> are graspable by the mind if and only if predicates of propositional attitude are projectible, predictive, well-behaved predicates of psychological theory.... The reason for this version of graspability is that Frege's demand that propositions be something the mind can grasp is

tantamount to the demand that propositions *make a difference* to the mind; that is to say, a creature's psychological state.

Dennett cites two classes of argument to the conclusion that these three conditions are jointly unsatisfiable: Putnam-style (1975a) twin-Earth arguments and Kaplan-style indexicality arguments. I will rehearse them very quickly, since I will return to arguments of this form in much more detail in chapter 5. In twin-Earth arguments, we are asked to imagine another planet, exactly like ours in every respect but one. Wherever H_2O is present on Earth, a macroscopically indistinguishable compound XYZ is present on Twin-Earth, called by Twin-English speakers "water". Since I believe *that water is H_2O*, so does Twin-Garfield. Psychologically, it would seem, we are twins, since we are physically twins (except for the presence of H_2O in my body wherever XYZ is present in his, which, *ex hypothesi*, makes no difference). But, whereas my belief is about water, and is true, his is about Twater, and is false. Hence we have different propositional attitudes, and hence we are related to distinct propositions. The conclusion drawn by Putnam and Dennett, among others, is that whatever it is that the mind grasps (apparently the same thing in both of us) is not the same as the intension-determiner/truth-value-bearer.

Kaplan's examples involve beliefs containing indexicals, such as "It is now 3:00." Again, presumably whenever two native speakers of English each have a belief that they would naturally express in these words their respective minds are in the same psychological state (in some relevant sense). But if they happen to have the belief at different times, they are related to different propositions if propositions that differ in truth value are necessarily distinct. Hence, what the mind grasps cannot be simultaneously psychologically and semantically active.

As Dennett notes, considerations such as these have led philosophers of a functionalist persuasion, and philosophically sensitive cognitive scientists, to recast the traditional model of a PA as an attitude not *immediately* to a proposition but rather, if to a proposition at all, only mediately, via a *sentence*, represented internally. Thus, propositional attitudes, on this model, are more accurately characterized as *sentential* attitudes. The most prominent champion of such a strategy has been Fodor, who in 1978 outlined a number of conditions to be met by any theory of PAs in preparation for arguing that only a sentential-attitude analysis is possible:

I. Propositional attitudes should be analyzed as relations. In particular, the verb in a sentence like "John believes it's raining" expresses a relation between John and something else, and a token of that sentence is true if John stands in the belief-relation to that thing.

II. A theory of PAs should explain the parallelism between verbs of PA and verbs of saying.

III. A theory of propositional attitudes should account for their opacity.

IV. The objects of propositional attitudes should have logical form.

V. A theory of propositional attitudes should mesh with empirical accounts of mental processes. (in Fodor 1981, pp. 178–186)

The argument to the conclusion that PAs are relations to internal representations that are sentential in form is then straightforward. It has the form of an argument from plausibility, that is, to the effect that such an account of PAs meets all five conditions, and a contention that no rival account is in sight. Suppose that our intentional phenomena are instantiated as states of our central nervous system that can be described as tokens of an internal language of thought (for our present purpose it doesn't matter whether this is a special "mentalese" or an internal system for representing tokens in a natural language, though since Fodor [1979] has argued for the mentalese alternative I will stick with that version). Then we can show how naturally all five conditions are met.

First, note that on this analysis the PAs are relational in a very straightforward sense. To believe that p is to represent in a particular way (presumably one peculiar to belief, as opposed to desire or hope) some internal token whose meaning is p. In virtue of being related in the appropriate way to that token, I believe that p. The parallelism between verbs of saying and the PA verbs is easy to explain on this model as well. The parallels in question are both semantic and syntactic: Both sets of verbs take *that*-clauses as complements; both are of a semantic type that (roughly, depending upon the details of one's semantic theory) corresponds to a function from propositions and individuals to propositions; both sets of verbs are non-truth-functional. These parallels would not be at all surprising on a Fodorian model, since on this account the PAs, like overt utterances, are biologically instantiated relations of individuals to concrete inscriptions of sentence tokens. That one set of relations is more readily observable than another should not be expected, *ceteris paribus*, to make any syntactic or semantic difference.

Opacity and logical form fall out easily, too, for on this account the immediate contents of PAs are concrete inscriptions of sentences. Since any individual referred to by any referring term in an internal sentence token is, *ipso facto*, referred to under a description, any two internal sentence tokens that referred to that same individual under different descriptions would be distinct tokens and hence relata of distinct beliefs. Hence, even beliefs relating two believers to the some individual, ascribing to that individual the same property but for each believer via distinct descriptions, are distinct beliefs. Hence, it is always fallacious to infer from the fact that S believes $F(a)$ and from the fact that $a = b$ that S believes $F(b)$. Similarly, the fact that the internal representations that are the immediate objects of thought on this account are sentential in form guarantees that they are suitable objects for propositional and quantificational logics, and hence that they can enter into deductive relationships.

The fifth condition is at the same time the hardest and the easiest for such a theory to meet. It is the hardest because it is the one condition that cannot be demonstrated to be met by philosophical reflection alone. It is always conceivable that, despite the best philosophical motivation for an account of the PAs, developments in psychology could force us to adopt another theory. At the same time, the currently tentative state of the psychology of cognition is such that no current theory places very serious constraints on philosophical theorizing in this domain. Given the dominant computational paradigm, however, this much can be said for the sentential approach: It seems a plausible account of how current computing machines are subjects of PAs (to the extent that PA attributions are appropriate for them), and if we take seriously the functional models of the mind-body relation we have seen to be induced by contemporary cognitive theory, and are realistic in our interpretation of PA ascriptions, it is hard to see how the internal states we posit could fail to have such sentential structure.

A possibly serious problem for accounts like Fodor's—according to which the PA predicates appear to function as predicates ranging over tokens of internal sentences—is raised by Thomason's (1977) argument. Thomason, generalizing a result of Montague (1963), argues that certain indirect discourse operators, such as "knows," cannot be interpreted as predicates ranging over sentence names (including sentence quotations) on pain of paradox, and it is at least plausible that on Fodor's sentential analysis the PA verbs receive just this interpretation. However, it is not clear that Thomason's result is immediately problematic for Fodor, even if the only plausible interpretation of his theory assigns this syntactic type to PA verbs. Thomason's result applies only to operators that have modal properties akin to "necessarily," properties that arguably attach to such terms as "knows" or "is trivial" but which do not plausibly attach to what Fodor calls the "pure" PA predicates (such as "believes" or "fears"), to which he restricts his account. (Indeed, this observation might suggest that Thomason's result could serve as a clue to demarcating the "pure" from the "impure" PA predicates, if one accepted that distinction.) However, in chapter 5 I will argue that Fodor is unable to maintain the distinction between the allegedly individualistically characterizable pure PAs and those requiring naturalistic accounts, such as "knows," and that all PAs are naturalistically infected. This suggests that there might be a generalization of Thomason's result showing that any analysis such as Fodor's is beset by paradox. If there is such a generalization, however, in light of the logical dissimilarities between "believes" and "knows," it is far from trivial. I shall reject Fodor's account on other (perhaps ultimately related) grounds.

This sentential-attitude account is meant to provide an analysis whereby there is a sense in which the mind grasps a truth-value bearer composed of extension determiners, hence meeting the apparently inconsistent demands of the Fregean triad noted by Dennett. The "grasping" relation is instantiated by the representation of the sentential token by the believer in the way peculiar to belief; the lexical components of the represented token in fact determine, in context, the reference of the referring terms in the embedded sentence in any correct belief attribution, and finally, as we shall see presently, in virtue of the fact that these states are typed by reference to their *contents*, there is a relatively clear sense in which, if the account is correct, in virtue of standing in the appropriate psychological relation to a token of a sentence, the subject of a PA stands in a cognitive relation to a *content*, that is, a proposition, which is the primary bearer of truth value. Whether this claim to satisfy the Fregean triad can in fact survive close scrutiny will emerge in chapter 5.

But despite the view the PAs are *instantiated* as relations to internal sentence tokens, the sententialist model of the PAs proposes, particularly in Fodor's and Pylyshyn's hands (but also for any supporter of the reality of the PAs in the cognitive framework), to *individuate* PAs by reference to their content, and herein, we will see, lies the source of the difficulty for PAs in the cognitive paradigm. Fodor is explicit about this:

> We were driven to functionalism ... by the suspicion that there are empirical generalizations about mental states that can't be formulated in the vocabulary of neurological or physical theories ... *all* of them are generalizations that apply to propositional attitudes in virtue of the content of the propositional attitudes.... Seeing that *a* is *F* is a normal cause of believing that *a* is *F*; ... statements that *p* are normally caused by beliefs that *p*; ... and so on and on.... [O]ur attempts at a serious cognitive psychology are founded in the hope that *this kind* of generalization can be systematized and made rigorous.... And: YOU CAN'T SAVE THESE GENERALIZATIONS WITHOUT APPEALING TO THE NOTION OF THE CONTENT OF A MENTAL STATE, since, as previously remarked, these generalizations are precisely such as apply to mental states in virtue of their contents. (1981, pp. 25–26)

On this model, which is clearly a (relatively) conservative refinement of the concept of belief in folk psychology, what we then need to do is to sketch a theory of what it is to identify a subject's belief by reference to its content. Stich's (1983) compelling account and that of Lycan (1983) form the basis for my own account. With this account in hand, I will be in a position to highlight the difficulties it poses for the integration of such a concept of belief into a computational psychology, preparatory to investigating strategies for surmounting them.

We are after a functionalist account of belief content—that is, one that will identify beliefs by reference to their roles in the *internal* economy of the believer. For instance, a crude model whereby for S to believe that p is for S to have in his or her brain and inscription of some sentence meaning that p would be out of the question on two counts. In the first place, the mere inscription might be causally inert, and though in some sense it would be a representation of p (say, for a neurosurgeon examining it), it would not be a representation that p for S, in the way that the serial number of a computer, even if stamped on the backs of ROM chips, is not thereby represented by the machine. Second, it might be that S believes that p dispositionally— that although S does not store any token of p, S would, if asked, assent to p, and exhibits all the behavior of one who believes that p. It might be, for instance, that S believes that q, and that $q \Rightarrow p$, and that S represents that entailment explicitly and can be counted upon to draw the obvious conclusion.

Now, in ascribing contentful states to our fellows we use sentences employing PA clauses. In doing so, we effectively exhibit the embedded complement clauses of the attitude verbs as instances of sentences that have the same content as the sentence embedded in the state we are ascribing to the subject in question. (This story is familiar from Sellars [1956, 1980, 1981] and from Davidson [1969, 1970, 1974, 1975].) The obvious question then is "What is it for two such sentences to have the same content?" As Stich points out, content identity is probably far too strong a condition here, given translation's ineliminable indeterminacy and its imprecision. Content *similarity* is a relation far better suited to the task of comparing beliefs to one another and to sentences in public languages. The question then gets rephrased: "What are the appropriate dimensions of similarity for beliefs?"

Stich suggests three dimensions, which, if they do not constitute an exhaustive list of such dimensions, at least do a pretty good job of capturing our pretheoretic notion of content similarity: *causal-pattern similarity*, *ideological similarity*, and *reference similarity*. Two beliefs are causal-pattern-similar to the extent that they have similar patterns of causal interaction with stimuli, behavior, and other psychological phenomena. This kind of similarity is at the core of the Sellarsian and functionalist idea that beliefs are similar to the extent that they play similar roles in the internal economies of their respective believers. But it is not the only dimension on which beliefs can be judged content-similar. If it were, we would run into trouble in the following kinds of cases.

Al and Bob each have a belief that they would express by saying "Smullyan is an important mathematician." Their beliefs were each caused by their having heard their respective teachers tell them "Smullyan is an important mathematician," and their beliefs have rather similar effects. Neither Al nor Bob knows the first name of the Smullyan whom he believes to be an important mathematician. Al's teacher was talking about Raymond, Bob's about Arthur. Hence, it would seem that Al believes that Raymond Smullyan is an important mathematician and Bob believes that Arthur is, though neither would be capable at this stage of his knowledge of expressing his belief in this detail. Hence, though their beliefs are causal-pattern-similar, they are not similar enough on all dimensions to be counted as the same belief on our ordinary belief taxonomy.

Calvin and Dave are very unlike one another. Calvin is deaf, mistrustful of persons in authority to the point of paranoia, and very reticent about revealing his true beliefs. Dave is blind, very trusting, and candid. Calvin is told (erroneously) in sign language by his teacher that Arthur Posterior did important work in logic. (He is told enough about him that only the actual Arthur Prior satisfies the description of "Arthur Posterior," and it was indeed Prior to whom his teacher intended to refer.) Dave reads in braille in *The Encyclopedia of Philosophy* that Arthur Prior did important work in logic. On the basis of these experiences, both Calvin and Dave form the belief that Arthur Prior did important work in logic, which causes Calvin, when asked the appropriate questions (in the presence of one in whom he does not have complete trust), to sign that Arthur Concurrent did important work in logic, and Dave to say that Arthur Prior did. Despite the considerable difference in the causal roles of these beliefs, there seems a strong sense in which they count as the same.

Al's and Bob's beliefs, while causal-pattern-similar and ideologically similar, are reference-dissimilar. That is, while their beliefs have very similar patterns of causal interaction, and while they are embedded in very similar contexts of other beliefs, desires, and other psychological states and processes (what ideological similarity comes to), they are referentially dissimilar. This is because the referents of the referring terms in the sentences they would use to express their beliefs are distinct. Reference similarity requires that the referents of the referring terms in subjects' belief-expression sentences be similar (typically, identical).

Calvin's and Dave's beliefs, while referentially very similar, are very dissimilar in the causal-pattern sense and the ideological sense. What is striking about their case is that, even though they differ most in just the two respects one might think *ab initio* are of the most interest to a cognitive psychology of belief (that is, in respect of their causal patterns and their ideological context), for many commonsense purposes we would attribute to them the same belief. This lack of fit between the internal state of the believer and the content of the beliefs will loom large in our framing of the problem of how to embed the PAs in psychology, as it does in Dennett's (1982) suspicions about the very reality of the PAs.

Also of interest here is the fact that belief identity is not only a matter of degree, in consequence of being really a similarity relation, but also (again issuing from its nature as a similarity relation) a matter of *perspective*. That is, depending upon what dimension is most interesting to you, you can come up with very different answers to the question "Do X and Y believe the same thing?" For there is surely a sense in which Al and Bob do believe the same thing, a sense that is useful in predicting and explaining their behavior. Similarly, if we want to predict and explain the behavior of Cal and Dave, there is a compelling sense in which the best thing to do is to ascribe to them very different beliefs,

This discussion has comprised a set of observations about the concept of belief as it functions in the manifest image. I have not attempted to craft a finely honed concept suitable for use in a scientific psychology. The question whether one can or must be crafted will come to center stage shortly. But with these sets of observations in hand, and with the outlines of a theory of what it is to ascribe a contentful state to a system *as contentful* in hand, and armed with our account of PAs as instantiated as sentential attitudes plus or minus a bit, we can begin to pose our problem. It will first be necessary to lay out some conditions on phenomena that would be useful to a scientific cognitive psychology.

The task of cognitive psychology is to characterize the structure of the human information processing system so as to provide an explanation of how we acquire, store, manipulate, and transform information, and of how we employ that information in guiding and producing behavior. It is, as such—*prima facie*, though perhaps not ultimately—a science of the internal workings of the individual organism. A way in which this point is frequently made involves what Stich calls the "autonomy principle":

> ... the states and processes that ought to be of concern to a psychologist are those that supervene on the current, internal, physical state of the organism.... What this amounts to is that any differences between organisms which do not manifest themselves as differences in their current, internal, physical states ought to be ignored by a psychological theory. If we respect the autonomy principle, then the fact that a pair of organisms have different histories or that they are in significantly different environments will be irrelevant to a psychological theory.... (1983, p. 164)

Stich argues for the autonomy principle using what he calls the replacement argument: In brief, if I were to be evaporated and replaced with a quark-for-quark replica of myself assembled in some other galaxy, with a history resembling mine in no respect, its psychology would be identical to mine, and any psychological phenomena relevant to an explanation of its behavior would be identical to any such phenomena relevant to an explanation of mine. Our different histories make no difference to our psychology, and if they do not, then no such extra-organismic variables can be relevant to an organism's psychology.

This is not, I believe, a terribly compelling argument for the autonomy principle as a general principle of psychological methodology, and it will come in for detailed criticism in chapter 6. For now I want to note that, given a faith in the neurobiological instantiation of the human information-processing system, it is at least highly plausible to suggest that the phenomena relevant to a specification of the properties of that system are supervenient upon those neurobiological states. Further credence is given to this view by the consideration that these states are those that are most immediately caused by the afferent impulses from sensory nerve bundles and are the proximal causes of the efferent impulses that give rise to motion. If one wanted to explain the processing of information originating in the senses and culminating in action, where better to look than the central nervous system for the relevant phenomena?

Finally, a consideration in favor of looking inside the skull for the individuating conditions of the phenomena of interest to psychology has to do with the hope that the predicates of a finished cognitive psychology will in some sense harmonize with those of a neuroscience. This harmony needn't, of course, be expressed in a replacement of the one by the other, or in a wholesale restatement of the generalizations of psychology in the language of neuroscience. But if one takes the model of systematic reduction offered in the preceding chapter seriously, then one is committed to the view that the reduction of a systematic explanation of the human information-processing system will eventually bottom out in an explanation of the instantiation of the elementary information processes of that system in some hardware, and the obvious hardware is the wetware of the human central nervous system. Thus, suggests this argument, if the explanations offered by cognitive psychology are genuinely information-processing explanations interpreted realistically, one would hope that the information processes they posit supervene only on the neurological states of the human nervous system.

· With these considerations in hand, we can pose the central problem of this investigation: It seems impossible that anything like the PAs as construed by the manifest image—that is, as individuated as contenful—can meet the conditions for psychological phenomena, because no phenomena individuated by content can satisfy the autonomy principle and no phenomena that violate the autonomy principle are suitable objects for psychology. Hence, it appears either that psychology must give up on explaining the PAs or that psychology cannot be a science. There are three tightly related motivations (or perhaps three ways of expressing the same motivation) for this problem.

The first reason is that, as we have seen in the foregoing discussion, assigning content to a psychological state requires attention to its context, as one of the critical dimensions of content similarity along which one must compare state contents is that of reference similarity. If the content of a psychological state is sensitive (as this suggests it is) to extra-organismic contributions, such phenomena violate the autonomy principle.

The second reason is that the notion of content is vague, and hence classes of states grouped by content for the purposes of standing under psychological generalizations will have vague membership conditions. The discussion of content similarity above made it clear that this relation is indeed, in virtue of being a similarity relation, both a matter of degree and subject to variations in the interests and perspective of the attitude ascriber. We have seen Stich and Churchland argue that for there to be psychological generalizations in a projectible vocabulary, there must be a fact of the matter as to whether a particular phenomenon satisfies any particular predicate in that vocabulary, and this decision should not depend upon the explanatory interest of a third party. Since, on the account sketched above, intentional ontological classes such as PAs have identity membership conditions that fail to be all-or-none and which depend upon what dimension of similarity is of importance to the classifier, they fail to constitute appropriate classes for a scientific psychology.

Finally, as a consequence of these two considerations, predicates whose extensions are determined by content ascriptions appear not to be projectible. All of the more fundamental sciences are cast in a physicalistic vocabulary, and there is good *prima facie* reason to believe that psychology should be embeddable in some sense (perhaps short of genuine reduction) in a more fundamental science such as neurobiology, as we have seen in the preceding arguments. At the very least one would expect that the IPS explanations offered by such a psychology would bottom out in an account of the neural instantiation of the most fundamental psychological properties. But if this is so, the higher-level properties of such a psychology would thus eventually have corresponding neurobiological properties in any particular organism—that is, properties the satisfaction of which, in particular organisms at particular times, constitute the satisfaction of its concurrent psychological properties—if not properties with which they would be necessarily coextensive. But if intentional predicates are both vague and nonautonomous, they can't have corresponding neural properties, since neural properties are determinate and autonomous. Thus, on this account, the intentional properties are nonprojectible and hence unsuited for a scientific psychology.

This, then, is the central problem. There is good reason to believe (1) that psychology should be individualistic (that is, should respect the autonomy principle) and precise, (2) that it should account for the PAs, and (3) that the PAs are nonindividualistic, vaguely characterized phenomena. But this is an inconsistent triad. Something must go. In the remainder of this chapter, I will explore two versions of each of two strategies. The first strategy, which I call the *reconciliationist* strategy, attempts to salvage (1) and (2) by providing an individualistic treatment of the PAs. The second, the *eliminativist* strategy, attempts to retain (1) and (3) while banishing the PAs from the ontology of psychology. Each strategy comes in both a solipsistic and a naturalistic version. In the two succeeding chapters I will argue that neither of these strategies can work, and that the correct solution lies in rejecting (1)—the assumption that psychology can be individualistic—and formulating a naturalistic psychology capable of explaining human intentional states.

Reconciliationist approaches comprise two specific proposals: Fodor's *Methodological Solipsism* and Pylyshyn's *Naturalistic Individualism*. Both propose to accommodate the PAs in the computational paradigm by identifying them with determinate, internal, computationally characterized states of the central nervous system. They diverge from each other in the degree to which they take distal information seriously in characterizing these states. In this section, I will outline Fodor's Methodological Solipsism.

It is useful to begin a discussion of Methodological Solipsism by distinguishing naturalistic from solipsistic methodologies in psychology. The distinction is originally due to James (1890), and was emphasized by Tolman (1922, 1936, 1948). A naturalistic psychology is one that posits and explains phenomena which are characterized in part with reference to relations the organism or its internal events, states, and processes bear to objects or events in the organism's history or environment. That is, such a psychology takes seriously the possibility that characterizing and typing phenomena for the purposes of psychology requires one to pay attention to relations between the organism and its environment. A solipsistic psychology, by contrast, characterizes its theoretical phenomena and explananda without regard to any phenomena outside the organism, or even, in an extreme version, to any phenomena outside of its central nervous system.

Fodor characterizes his Methodological Solipsism as follows:

> ... so long as we are thinking of mental processes as purely computational, the bearing of environmental information upon such processes is exhausted by the formal character of whatever the oracles

write on the tape. In particular, it doesn't matter to such processes whether what the oracles write is *true*; whether, for example, they really are transducers faithfully mirroring the state of the environment, or merely the output end of a typewriter manipulated by a Cartesian demon bent on deceiving the machine. I'm saying, in effect, that the formality condition, viewed in this context, is tantamount to a sort of methodological solipsism. If mental processes are formal, then they have access only to the formal processes of such representations of the environment as the senses provide. Hence they have no access to the *semantic* properties of such representations, including ... the property of being representations *of the environment*. (Fodor 1980 [in Fodor 1981, p. 231])

This methodological solipsism is meant to be conjoined with a representational theory of mind, and so is meant to be a methodology appropriate to explaining and characterizing representational phenomena, despite ignoring all semantic properties of those representations. This at least appears paradoxical, and in chapter 5 I will argue that it must prove incoherent. Let us now examine the account in detail, and the argument Fodor offers on its behalf.

The argument begins by noting that psychology in the computational paradigm requires that psychological phenomena satisfy what Fodor calls the "formality condition," i.e., that all psychological phenomena are represented as formally (that is, syntactically) defined objects, or computations over such objects, and that any two phenomena can differ in content (and hence in psychological type, since we are identifying such states as the PAs by content) only if they differ formally. As Fodor notes, this condition rules out as psychological predicates such factive predicates as "knows" and "sees that," since whether a state is a state of S knowing that p depends not only upon the formal characterization of the token represented in S's belief register but also upon whether p happens to be true. Fodor hence envisions a cleavage between the allegedly naturalistically infected commonsense psychological predicates (e.g. "knows") and the predicates allegedly not so infected (e.g. "believes"). Whether there are any such antiseptic predicates will emerge as a bone of contention in chapter 5.

Fodor takes work in artificial intelligence, and the fruitfulness of the computer metaphor in cognitive psychology, to be supportive of this methodological solipsism. This is not surprising, for it is natural to think of the representational states of computing machines and the processes that operate on them as, in the end, purely formal symbolic states and purely formal algebraic processes defined over them, respectively. The machine operates on them in a way that is absolutely indifferent to the semantic interpretation, if any, we operators impose on them. If human psycholog-

ical phenomena are interpreted as strictly analogous to machine representational states and processes, as they are on this construal of the computational paradigm, then it is natural to think of these human events, states,
and processes as obeying the same formality condition.

A further argument for construing the PAs solipsistically relies upon the
fact that, for the purposes of the explanation and prediction of behavior,
the only useful content taxonomy of such phenomena is one that assigns
them their types under an opaque construal of the attitudes. That is, from
the facts that John believes that $F(a)$ and that $a = b$, it does not follow that
John believes that $F(b)$. Fodor offers the following example:

> ... Suppose I know that John wants to meet the girl who lives next
> door, and suppose I know that this is true when "wants to" is con-
> strued opaquely. Then, given even rough-and-ready generalizations
> about how people's behaviors are contingent on their utilities, I can
> make some reasonable predictions (guesses) about what John is likely
> to do: he's likely to say (viz. utter), "I want to meet the girl who lives
> next door." ...
>
> On the other hand, suppose that all I know is that John wants to
> meet the girl next door where "wants to" is construed transparently;
> i.e., all I know is that it's true of the girl next door that John wants to
> meet her. Then there is little or nothing that I can predict about how
> John is likely to proceed. And this is *not* just because rough-and-ready
> psychological generalizations want *ceteris paribus* clauses to fill them
> in; it's also for the deeper reason that I can't infer from what I know
> about John to any relevant description of the mental causes of his
> behavior. For example, I have no reason to predict that John will say
> such things as, "I want to meet the girl who lives next door," since, let
> John be as cooperative and truthful as you like, and let him be utterly
> a native speaker, still, he *may* believe that the girl he wants to meet
> languishes in Latvia.... (Fodor 1980 [in Fodor 1981, p. 235])

Some refinements of Fodor's notion of opacity are necessary to make the
account tidy, essentially involving replacing it with a notion of nontrans-
parency; these needn't concern us here.)

The essential point to emerge from this argument and example is that in
any account of a representation of a proposition of the form $F(a)$ as the
content of a PA, two features of the representational states involved are
necessary: First, the representation to which the subject is related by the
attitude in question is a formal object in a determinate vocabulary assembled according to some formation rules (a straightforward consequence
of the formality condition). Second, as a consequence of this first feature,
the object(s) that constitute the referent(s) of the embedded sentence and
the set (or other semantic entity) that is the semantic value of the predicate

expression contained in the embedded sentence are both represented by the subject *under a description* and there is no freedom of substitutivity of co-referring expressions in the attitude ascription *for the purposes of psychology*. This is simply because the efficient causes of behavior and the effects of perception and other mental processes are the formal symbols and processes represented in the mind; different symbols can be expected, *ceteris paribus*, to have different characteristic causes and effects.

The central tenets of Fodor's Methodological Solipsism so far are these: Though psychological phenomena are to be identified and categorized by reference to their content, the content is *opaque* content. Differences in content are always reflected in differences in the form of the syntactic state underlying a representation. Finally, the only phenomena that are of interest to psychology are those solipsistically characterized states that are amenable such treatment (including the nonfactive PAs). The argument so far has been largely positive, to the effect that a solipsistic treatment of the attitudes is possible. The second part of Fodor's account is the argument that a naturalistic account of the attitudes is impossible:

> A naturalistic psychology would specify the relations that hold between an organism and an object in its environment when the one is thinking about the other. Now, think how such a theory would have to go. Since it would have to define its generalizations over mental states on the one hand and environmental entities on the other, it will need, in particular, some canonical way of referring to the latter. Well, *which* way? If one assumes that what makes my thought about Robin Roberts a thought *about Robin Roberts* is some causal connection between the two of us, then we'll need a description of RR such that the causal connection obtains in virtue of his satisfying that description. And *that* means, presumably, that we'll need a description under which the relation between him and me instantiates a law.
>
> ... But here's the depressing consequence again: we have no access to such a vocabulary prior to the elaboration (completion?) of the nonpsychological sciences. "What Granny likes with her herring" isn't, for example, a description under which salt is law-instantiating; nor, presumably, is "salt." What we need is something like "NaCl," and descriptions like "NaCl" are available only *after* we've done our chemistry. (Fodor 1980 [in Fodor 1981, p. 249])

The central claim of this argument is, of course, that the vocabulary of naturalistic generalizations could never be a scientific vocabulary. And this is because the predicates of such a vocabulary would necessarily have in their extensions not only psychological phenomena but environmental ones as well. If they are to range over environmental phenomena, then they are constrained by the categories of the more fundamental physical sciences. That is, on Fodor's account, a naturalistic psychology would include, *inter alia*, an account of the nomic generalizations in virtue of which environmental phenomena can be truly said to *cause* psychological phenomena. But such causal generalizations, like all causal generalizations about the interaction of physical objects, must be stated in the vocabulary of the theoretical physical sciences. These sciences, however, are not yet so complete that they provide us with a projectible description of any significant range of the phenomena that would figure in such a naturalistic psychology, and probably never will be. Hence, such a psychology cannot be constructed. Thus, Fodor concludes, since naturalistic psychology is impossible, and since Methodological Solipsism provides a plausible account of the PAs, Methodological Solipsism provides us with the only workable methodology for psychology and for an accommodation of the PAs therein.

I now wish to step back a bit from the text of Fodor's argument to offer a general characterization of the strategy Methodological Solipsism adopts for solving the problem of the accommodation of the PAs in psychology. The idea is this: The human IPS is first characterized as a formal symbol-manipulation system. This is done by arriving, through careful inspection of the interrelations of its internal neurobiological events, states, and processes, at a computational interpretation of those phenomena, much as one would arrive at an interpretation of a calculator's internal states if its symbols were entirely foreign and its internal workings unfamiliar. In arriving at this interpretation, we develop a theory of the internal code (the "language of thought") manipulated by our IPS, as well as of the functional architecture of the system itself. But this solipsistic interpretation makes no reference to any objects or properties of objects in the world outside the organism—it is nothing more than a coherent computational model of the physical architecture and tokens of the system.

However, given the general argument for a representational theory of mind, for the reality of the representations posited in such a model, and for the necessity of positing them in order to capture psychological generalizations, we will as yet, in virtue of having avoided a representational characterization of any of the internal events or processes of the IPS so far, be unable to say anything psychologically interesting. Thus, we interpret. In order to assign content to the system, and hence to arrive at psychologically useful words and generalizations, we imagine an interpretation of the system's language and architecture such that under this interpretation the system's behavior would make sense in an environment pretty much like the one we live in. In doing so, we remain solipsistic. We do not ask whether the internal events of the system were caused by or have effects on this environment. We do not inquire into the truth or falsity of the representations we ascribe to it. But if we are successful in constructing a model such as this, we will have arrived at a description of the system in terms of which we can explain its behavior as rational and hence vindicate our interpretation of it as a representational system.

On this account, for such a system (like us) to have a PA is for it to represent in an appropriate way—that is, to be in an appropriate computational state with respect to—a symbol sequence that bears under the appropriate interpretive scheme the interpretation (opaquely construed) of the embedded content sentence of the PA ascription. The account is reconciliationist in that, if it were to succeed, it would preserve both the essential features of the computational paradigm and the reality of the PAs; it is individualistic in that it identifies the PAs with internal states of their subjects; and it is solipsistic in that on this account PAs can be identified and attributed in the absence of any information about their subjects' environments, histories, or relations to their environments. (These are distinct points. The solipsism in methodological solipsism is an epistemological matter—a commitment to the dispensability in principle, if not necessarily in practice, of information concerning the subject's environment and his or her relations to it; the individualism is an ontological matter— a commitment to the view that a subject's psychological state is to be identified with his or her nonrelational physical states.)

In the next chapter, I will argue that Methodological Solipsism cannot work as an analysis of the PAs or as a methodology for psychology. For now, however, it is sufficient to characterize this attempt at a solution to the problem posed by the PAs for psychology. We will now consider a contrasting naturalistic solution within the reconciliationist framework: Pylyshyn's naturalistic individualism.

It may be somewhat unfair or inaccurate to attribute the Naturalistic Individualism I will characterize to Pylyshyn. His own statements of his position (Pylyshyn 1984) are somewhat vague, and at times he seems to believe (despite, I think, clear differences between the two positions) that he is a Fodorian methodological solipsist. Nonetheless, even if the view I attribute to Pylyshyn is at odds with his views, the Naturalistic Individualism I will characterize is, I would argue, the dominant metatheoretic view of psychologists working in the cognitive paradigm—even if it does not accurately characterize their actual scientific or theoretical practice. (See Burge 1987; Stillings 1987; Marr 1982. Such a view is also urged by Bach [1982] and McGinn [1982] in the philosophical literature.)

Pylyshyn contrasts his Naturalistic Individualism with Methodological Solipsism (actually, the intended contrast is with Stich's Eliminativist Computationalism, but the critical feature of the theory at issue is the solipsism which Stich and Fodor share) in the story of Mary, which I repeat here for convenience:

It simply will not do as an explanation of, say, why Mary came running out of a certain smoke-filled building, to say that there was a certain sequence of expressions computed in her mind according to certain expression-transforming rules. However true that might be, it fails on a number of counts to provide an explanation of Mary's behavior. It does not show how or why this behavior is related to very similar behavior she would exhibit as a result of receiving a phone call in which she heard the utterance "this building is on fire!", or as a consequence of her hearing the fire alarm, or smelling smoke, or in fact following any event interpretable as generally entailing that the building was on fire. The only way to both capture the important underlying generalizations ... is to ... [interpret] the expressions in the theory as goals and beliefs....

Of course the computational [methodologically solipsistic] model only contains uninterpreted formal symbols.... The question is whether the cognitive theory which that model instantiates can refrain from giving them an intentional [meaningful] interpretation. In the above example, leaving them as uninterpreted formal symbols simply begs the question of why these particular expressions should arise under what would surely seem (in the absence of interpretation) like a very strange collection of diverse circumstances, as well as the question of why these symbols should lead to building evacuation as opposed to something else.... What is common to all of these situations is that a common interpretation of the events occurs.... But what in the theory corresponds to this common interpretation? Surely one cannot answer by pointing to some formal symbols. *The right answer has to be something like the claim that the symbols represent the belief that the building is on fire....* (Pylyshyn 1980, p. 161; emphasis mine)

The point of this argument is fairly straightforward. A good cognitive explanation of behavior that is motivated by beliefs ought to explain how those beliefs are related to the behavior and to the circumstances that give rise to them. If the beliefs are ultimately characterized by the theory as uninterpreted symbols, and if believing is ultimately characterized as an uninterpreted process in the believer, then the theory can't explain their connection either to behavior or to stimulation (or, for that matter, to other beliefs). Now, as we have seen, according to Methodological Solipsism, PAs do in the end get characterized as contentful representational states, and the generalizations that Methodological Solipsism envisions for a psychology of such states are couched in the language of representation and content. But what is important to remember, and what distinguishes Methodological Solipsism from Naturalistic Individualism, is that according

to Methodological Solipsism the content of these states is a function solely
of their relations to one another, and not of their relations to the external
world (which can safely be ignored).

In any real explanation of behavior such as Mary's, Pylyshyn's argument
goes, the content of the belief as determined by its causal and semantic
connections to her environment plays a role. The symbols in Mary's head
cause her behavior *because* they represent the fact that there is fire, and any
symbols that did not represent that fact would, by themselves, not explain
her behavior. And further, their representing fire consists in and can only be
explained by the relationships that obtain between them and instances of
fire. Computational states not so hooked up with combustion, whatever
their connections with other states and however possible it would be to
construct a coherent model of Mary's behavior in which they did represent
fire, would not represent fire. Hence, the fact that a psychological state can
be coherently assigned a particular "content" by a solipsistic theorist does
not entail the correctness of that content ascription. Naturalistic relations
are necessary as well. (Compare Putnam's [1981] discussion of reference
and the "brain in a vat" hypothesis, which I discuss in chapter 5.) The
conclusion is that in cognitive theory, internal information-processing
states have to be identified by their content (this is what makes the position
reconciliationist, and this is where Naturalistic Individualism and Methodological Solipsism converge), and that in order to do this one must examine
their connections not only to other cognitive states and processes but also
to the organism's distal environment (this is what makes Naturalistic Individualism naturalistic, and where Naturalistic Individualism and Methodological Solipsism diverge). It is important, however, to not that, despite
the naturalism with respect to the facts that determine interpretation, this
strategy is thoroughly individualistic in its account of the nature of the
states that "get interpreted." They are construed as purely internal. (Davidson [1987] adopts a version of this view.) Pylyshyn puts it this way:

> The basic problem is that *representing* is a semantic relation.... It
> may be that representation requires that certain causal relations with
> the world were established at some point in the organism's history.
> For example, in order to represent the sensory feature *red* as a par-
> ticular sensory quality, some aspect of the sensory state must be
> causally related to an occasion on which the organism was in sensory
> contact with a color in the category red....
>
> ... the relation of representing is taken as arising from the role of
> the functional state within the complete theory, *including the way the
> organism interacts with its environment* [emphasis mine] through ...
> transducers, the way it relates to those of its inputs and outputs that

are considered to be interpreted ... and the relation of the organism's behavior and its own history of such interactions [sic]. (1984, p. 42)

One further way of getting at the distinction between Methodological Solipsism and Naturalistic Individualism is by considering that if one takes these arguments seriously, Naturalistic Individualism questions the very coherence of the solipsistic strategy. Methodological Solipsism insists that information-processing states and processes are to be taken, *ab initio*, by cognitive theory as *uninterpreted, formal* states and processes, and that they are to be identified without paying attention to any relations between the organism and the environment. Now, the naturalist, armed with the considerations raised above about the necessary conditions of justifiable interpretation, can argue as follows: We agree with the Methodological Solipsist that information-processing states are not to be identified *physically*, for then we could not generalize about information-processing systems realized in physically different substrata, such as persons and artificially intelligent but perhaps functionally equivalent computers. But here is the challenge to Methodological Solipsism: Given something you have reason to believe is an information-processing system (perhaps because it is a living, functioning adult human being) and whose behavior you wish to explain as a cognitive scientist, you have the task of deciding which of its *physical* states and processes are going to count as *functional* or *computational* states and processes. And because you don't even know which kinds of neural phenomena to begin *interpreting*, you can't just stare at the neurons and figure it out. Naturalistic Individualism proposes that in order to accomplish this interpretive task it is necessary to watch the organism interact with the environment, and see how the neural stuff acts when confronted with particular types of stimulation, when the organism performs certain kinds of action and solves certain kinds of problems, and to interpret the states accordingly. And that is a naturalistic strategy (an epistemological strategy, not an ontological thesis—naturalistic individualism, despite its epistemological naturalism, is an ontologically individualistic position). But anything less would leave one with data that, in virtue of ignoring the connections between the organism's internal states and processes and the environment, would underdetermine the interpretation of its internal events, states, and processes (and would probably even fail to determine which of the countless ways of cataloging the set of physical parameters descriptive of its internal constitution are relevant to psychology).

The point here is that just to make the initial move from the physical level of description to the functional or computational level (as we must in order to interpret representational phenomena realistically in psychology at all) is to interpret the system, and the only way to get the data that justify a particular interpretation is to pay attention to naturalistic phenomena. So the methodological solipsist, on this account, is wrong in two ways: First, he is wrong in thinking that there is such a thing as an uninterpreted formal description of a natural physical system, for whenever we describe a naturally occurring system as an instance of a formal system we are thereby interpreting its components as tokens of formal types. Second, he is wrong in thinking that solipsistic data alone could justify even a minimal interpretation of the states of a physical system as information-processing states.

There is a final line of argument that distinguishes Naturalistic Individualism from Methodological Solipsism. Naturalistic Individualism charges Methodological Solipsism with being ultimately unable to support a realism about the psychological phenomena its theories posit—Methodological Solipsism, the Naturalistic Individualist can argue, is committed to the interpretation of psychological states as PAs (and *mutatis mutandis* for other contentful phenomena) solely by reference to the relations they bear to one another. Suppose it were possible, independent of any naturalistic evidence, to identify all the relevant events, states, and processes, and to interpret them. Given the existence of any one such solipsistic interpretation, there are (as was noted above) guaranteed to be indefinitely many equally good but mutually incompatible interpretations. The only credentials one could adduce in favor of any one interpretation over another, in the absence of naturalistic evidence, would be usefulness or convenience to the theorist. But this would leave open the question of what the *subject* of the representational phenomena in question actually represents by means of them. There would, on such a methodology, be no distinction possible between a theorist's interpretation of a state and the content of that state. All content ascriptions, on this account, would be capable of merely instrumental interpretation. But, claims the naturalist, given the context in which psychological phenomena actually occur, they have (at least relatively) determinate contents. If we pay attention to these interactions, we can determine what the *actual content for the subject* of the states in question is. This allows us to discriminate between assignments of content that have a claim to reality—that actually explain the subject's behavior and its connection both to internal representations and to the world—and those that, although perhaps of use to a theorist, fail to explain the observed behavior of the subject in context. Without these naturalistic data to constrain interpretation, indeterminacy runs wild. (See Pylyshyn 1984, esp. pp. 43–48.)

This characterization of Naturalistic Individualism completes my discussion of the two reconciliationist approaches to the PAs. It is important to note that, despite the naturalism of Naturalistic Individualism, both approaches are individualist in character—both identify such contentful states as the PAs with internal computational states of the human IPS (and therefore, ultimately, with token neurophysiological states). It is the hope of those who endorse these reconciliationist programs that these token states can satisfactorily be identified—albeit with suitable theoretical refinement—with the commonsense states of folk psychology, viz., beliefs, desires, hopes, and fears. The only difference between them, and we will see that in the end it is a minor though highly suggestive one, is the degree to which they take seriously the embedding of the organism in the environment. In the next chapter, after we survey the eliminativist approaches to the PAs, we will see that the naturalism that motivates Naturalistic Individualism in the end spells the incoherence not only of Methodological Solipsism but, when taken seriously, of Naturalistic Individualism as well.

Like the reconciliationist approach to the problem of the place of the PAs in cognitive psychology, the eliminativist approach divides along naturalist/solipsist lines (though the relation between the dichotomy in the case of eliminativist approaches and that in the case of the reconciliationist approaches might not be clear until the end of the discussion). Both versions of eliminativism are committed to the view that the PAs are to be understood as the theoretical posits of an ultimately false theory—"folk psychology" (Stich 1983) or the "person-theory" (Churchland 1979)—and are to be jettisoned with that theory in favor of the nonintentional, nonrepresentational posits of successor psychologies (computational for Stich, neurological for Churchland). Stich's is the solipsist version, and it is his argument I will articulate in some detail in this section. He calls his view the "syntactic theory of the mind." In order to emphasize its place amid the space of plausible solutions to the problem of the PAs, I will refer to it as "Eliminative Computationalism."

Stich argues that no ontology of the mental suitable for psychology can be committed to the existence of any phenomena sharing the intentional, representational properties of the PAs, and that, inasmuch as psychology is the final arbiter of the ontology of the mental, the consequence of this failure of the PAs to appear in its ontology entails their nonexistence. Our belief (if I may use this word in this context) in belief and its cousin states and processes is to be explained by our vestigial commitment to the demonstrably false folk-psychological theory on which we have been raised. As this theory is supplanted by a well-developed cognitive psychology, Stich argues, we will cease to believe in belief. Throughout the discussion of the eliminativist views we will assume the accuracy of the characterization of the PAs (taken from Stich 1983) offered earlier in this chapter. The argument will be that nothing satisfying any conditions remotely like those outlined in that account (individuated by causal-role, ideological, and/or reference similarity, or any other plausible conditions of content identity) could serve as the theoretical entities of a well-developed psychology.

Stich distinguishes between two forms that the commitment to the existence of such phenomena takes: the strong and weak Representational Theories of Mind. They differ from one another in that, whereas the strong Representational Theory of Mind requires that psychological generalizations characterize and explain psychological phenomena in terms of their contents (a view endorsed by Pylyshyn and Fodor, among others), the weak Representational Theory of Mind (also endorsed by Fodor in certain passages) allows that psychological generalizations can be stated over syntactically individuated phenomena, but requires that each of these phenomena also have a description as representational and that all such generalizations can be restated in representational language. Inasmuch as Stich (1983, pp. 207–208) correctly points out that all arguments against the strong Representational Theory of Mind and in favor of the superiority of Eliminative Computationalism apply *mutatis mutandis* to the weak Representational Theory of Mind, I will consider only the strong version of that thesis here. I will then turn to Stich's contrastive development of Eliminative Computationalism as a positive alternative.

The strong Representational Theory of Mind, as we have seen, is "the claim that cognitive science seeks (or ought to seek) generalizations which relate mental state types in virtue of their contents" (Stich 1983, p. 129). Stich argues that there are three reasons to be suspicious of such a theory: that the theory requires individuation on the basis of what is at bottom a similarity relation (that of content identity); that the exemplar which forms the basis of the similarity relation is a state of the attributer and hence builds "observer relativity" (ibid., p. 136) into psychological theory; and that such dimensions as reference and ideological similarity will often be beside the point when we are trying to individuate psychological phenomena on a basis that will allow the prediction and explanation of behavior, where causal-disposition similarity is all that counts. These last two difficulties are, of course, rooted in the first, and to expose them we will consider how each of the similarity dimensions relevant to belief identifications raises difficulties for the Representational Theory of Mind. In each case, as we will see, the point is that the culprit is the nonindividualistic nature of content ascriptions.

On this account, ideological similarity poses problems for content individuation because of the possibility of dramatic ideological differences between putative believers and belief ascribers. Two beliefs are ideologically similar to the extent that they occupy similar addresses in similar doxastic neighborhoods. Suppose I, as a cross-cultural cognitive psychologist, attempt to assign a belief to a member of a culture whose citizens have radically different basic beliefs about the world. I will have to settle upon some content sentence by means of which to identify his belief. That sentence will have to be one that is the content of a state of mine that occupies a similar ideological position in me to the state of my subject. But there might be none. In such cases, whether candidate believers have any beliefs, and, if so, what beliefs they have, would, on this account, depend critically on who is the belief ascriber. But this seems wrong, and what seems to be at the root of the problem is the use of content as the individuating category. And the reason that individuation by content issues in this ineliminable relativity is that ascriptions of content identity are always really ascriptions of content similarity, and the second relatum of the similarity relation is always a state of the belief ascriber. These problems, as Stich points out, do not require us to imagine exotic cultures in order to foresee. The ideologies of small children, the deranged, and the religiously, philosophically, or politically fanatical may pose similar problems for belief ascription.

The referential dimension also raises the possibility of there being no preferred or even plausible content sentence with which to ascribe a belief to one who would appear to be a believer. Stich's tale of Mr. Binh (repeated here for convenience) will serve to illustrate this point:

> ... Suppose that our subject, a Mr. Binh, is a recent immigrant to the United States whose mastery of English is rather shaky. A bright and attentive man, Binh is anxious to learn as much as possible about his adopted country. On his first day off the plane, he overhears a conversation about a Mr. Jefferson, whose exploits are of obvious interest to the people on whom he is eavesdropping. Unknown to Binh, the people whose conversation he overhears are avid TV fans, and they are discussing the most recent travails of the fictional black dry-cleaning magnate.... Binh takes it all in. The next day, Binh begins citizenship classes and he hears that Jefferson was a statesman, an inventor, and a major figure in the early history of America. Binh remembers, though he does not suspect that his teacher may be referring to a different Jefferson. On the third day Binh hears some discussion of a Mr. Feferman, a brilliant logician. However, with his ear not yet well attuned to spoken English, Binh hears "Feferman" as "Jefferson." Finally, on the fourth day, Binh meets an old friend and has a long chat about what he has learned of his new country. "I am," he says, "very anxious to learn more about this fascinating fellow Jefferson, the black patriot and statesman who made significant contributions to logic while building a dry-cleaning empire." (Stich 1983, pp. 145–146)

Now, what content sentence could we possibly use in the characterization of Binh's doxastic state? The reason that there is no really good candidate is that any plausible candidate would involve some use of "Jefferson" as a referring expression. It seems to function that way for Binh. But to whom does it refer? Any belief of ours that we would characterize in which that name would function referentially would hardly be similar to Binh's— certainly not similar enough to warrant a claim that they were identical. But it would seem to follow from this line of argument that Binh has no belief, which seems absurd. The problem seems, Stich argues, to stem from the identification of individual cognitive states (of which we and Binh clearly have plenty, some of which may be similar on psychologically interesting dimensions) by means of referential relations which may be wildly different, or which may even misfire completely.

Causal-similarity relations play similar havoc with belief ascriptions. It is plausible that the doxastic-perceptual-motor networks of the very young, the senile, the deranged, and the retarded are quite different from our own. One way of putting that is that the states that would seem to be *prima facie* candidates for identification as beliefs might all have typical causes and typical effects quite dissimilar from any states of ours to which we attribute content. If this were the case, then, just as with the problems caused by ideological and referential similarity, the causal-potential similarity dimension would render the task of belief individuation by content assignment in such candidate believers hopeless.

The last of the difficulties that Stich raises for the Representational Theory of Mind that we will consider before sketching the positive proposal represented by Eliminative Computationalism is the problem posed by infralinguals. The problem is this: There appears to be strong *prima facie* evidence that there is significant neurobiological, ethological, and cognitive continuity between, on the one hand, infants, children, and adult humans, and, on the other, between the higher apes and humans. But on the account of the PAs we have adopted, given the great gulf between our ideology and the "ideologies" (if that word can coherently be applied in this case) of infants and chimpanzees, given the gulf between the causal connections between our psychological states and processes and theirs, and given the fact that they do not even use language to characterize their own internal psychological states or processes (and in fact may not even conceptualize them at all), there seems no possibility of attributing PAs to them. But this seems to introduce a fundamental ontological and methodological discontinuity where there ought to be continuity. We will consider a similar objection raised by Churchland below.

In view of these difficulties for the Representational Theory of Mind and hence for the utility of concepts like those of the PAs in psychology, Stich concludes that the theory in which the PA terms are embedded—folk psychology—represents a doomed and degenerate research program. Its degeneration leaves us no option but to reject its theoretical vocabulary and ontology, and to characterize an ontology of psychology devoid of the entities and individuative principles that led to the demise of folk psychology. And it has been the burden of the arguments recounted that at the core of all of the problems plaguing folk psychology is the individuation of psychological phenomena by reference to their content. Accordingly, the view with which Stich intends to replace Representational Theory of Mind is conspicuous in its denial of the reality of any intentional phenomena, including the PAs.

Stich's initial characterization of Eliminative Computationalism is as follows:

> The basic idea of the STM [Eliminative Computationalism] is that the cognitive states whose interaction is (in part) responsible for behavior can be systematically mapped to abstract syntactic objects in such a way that causal interactions among cognitive states, as well as causal links with stimuli and behavioral events, can be described in terms of the syntactic properties and relations of the abstract objects to which the cognitive states are mapped.... If this is right, then it will be natural to view cognitive state tokens as tokens of abstract syntactic objects. (Stich 1983, p. 149)

The crucial thing about the characterization of psychological phenomena on Eliminative Computationalism is that their characterization as *syntactic* explicitly precludes their characterization as *semantic*. That is, the phenomena relevant to the psychological explanation of behavior and cognition are characterized, in order to be explicable *qua* psychological, as uninterpreted tokens of a formal system whose formal properties are isomorphic to the relevant causal properties of the neurological phenomena within the central nervous system.

On this view, the enterprise of psychology looks something like this: The theorist hypothesizes the existence of a network of syntactically characterized but uninterpreted phenomena which are causally responsible for the control of behavior and the processing of perceptual information (hence including some hypothesis about the transduction of sensation to syntactic object, and syntactic object to movement). This is just the process of hypothesizing the existence of an IPS with a particular computational structure, but with no referential semantics. Once the specification of this hypothesized IPS is complete, the theorist can test generalizations couched in the vocabulary of the syntactic IPS, refining hypotheses about its structure as performance data demand. Effort would also be expended in the direction of determining the nature of the neurological-syntactic correspondence, whose nature, given the abstract characterization of the psychological theory, could be left largely open at the outset but would gradually become more accessible as the details of the structure of the IPS became more evident.

Such an account is both solipsistic and eliminative with respect to the PAs. Its solipsism is motivated explicitly by the replacement argument for the autonomy principle we discussed above. The replacement argument has as its conclusion that the only phenomena relevant to a scientific psychology are those that supervene on individual organisms under individualistic descriptions. Legal obligations, states of knowledge, relations to one's community, and other phenomena that supervene on a broader base of physical and social properties of the world, Stich argues, are to be construed as "hybrid" states, composed both of psychologically relevant internal syntactic states and of much that is irrelevant to psychology. Thus, for instance, we should not expect a psychological explanation of how one comes to own property, though this state might involve some psychological components.

Inasmuch as the content of an intentional state such as a PA depends not only on the syntactically characterized neurological state of the subject of that PA but also on the beliefs of the ascriber (in virtue of the lack of any criterion of content identity, as opposed to content similarity), on the referential context in which the believer and the utterer find themselves (in virtue of the relevant dimensions of similarity), and on other such things, contentful states find themselves in violation of the autonomy principle. Predicates ranging over such states are hence not candidates for the vocabulary of psychology. And since psychology is the science responsible for the ontology of the mental, the conclusion to be drawn from the fact that a psychology more correct than the folk theory it replaces has no room for belief (a theoretical entity in the domain of the old folk psychology) is that there is no such thing as belief. On Stich's view, individualism and eliminativism go hand in hand. (Although in chapter 6 I will find much in Stich's account with which to quarrel, this last observation, about the inseparability of individualism and the elimination of the PAs from the ontology of the mental, I believe, is correct, and lies at the base of the incoherence of Fodor's Methodological Solipsism, though I also believe that, when pressed, it is a point against Eliminative Computationalism as well.)

What happens to the PAs, and to explanations of behavior and cognitive performance that apparently advert to them, on Eliminative Computationalism? The answer to the first part of this question is, of course, that the PAs disappear as the discarded legacy of a superseded theory. On this account, all apparent explanations that make use of PA locutions or other such intentionally laden language are pseudo-explanations, belonging in the same bag as putative explanations of thermodynamic phenomena that make reference to caloric fluid. But, Stich argues, we lose none of the explanatory power that those who press the cause of intentional explanatory idioms are after. An argument of Fodor's is pressed into service to make this point: On Fodor's account (or at least on one version thereof), what makes the computational model of the mind capable of explaining behavior solipsistically is that differences between psychological phenomena in content are mirrored in differences of syntactic form. Differences in syntactic form are reflected, of course, in differences in physical characteristics. And it is in virtue of these physical characteristics that psychological phenomena have the causal powers in virtue of which they arise as a consequence of sensation (or from other psychological processes) and issue in movement (or in other psychological phenomena). Now, Stich, in defense of the equivalence in explanatory power of Eliminative Computationalism to that purported to be achieved by Methodological Solipsism or Naturalistic Individualism through their allegedly spurious positing of the PAs, points out that if one accepts Fodor's solipsism (for which, as we have seen, Stich argues on independent grounds) then the contentful characterization of any psychological phenomenon is a fifth wheel in the explanation; all of the genuine explanatory burden is borne by the physical and syntactic characterizations in virtue of which the states are active and theoretically accessible, respectively. At best, the contentful characterization of these computational phenomena is a gratuitous redescription; at worst, it is a misleading or misguided attribution of an essentially contentful character to what is, *qua* psychological, nonintentional.

Eliminative Computationalism hence shares with Methodological Solipsism, and not with Naturalistic Individualism, the property of being solipsistic—of treating psychological phenomena as essentially determinate phenomena that supervene on the internal constitution of individual organisms *and that can be identified and attributed while ignoring those organisms' environments or histories.* Eliminative Computationalism differs markedly from both Methodological Solipsism and Naturalistic Individualism in its eliminative character. Whereas both Methodological Solipsism and Naturalistic Individualism attempt to reconcile the PAs with the cognitive paradigm by embedding them within it, by offering a cognitive analysis of what it is to be in a PA, and by demonstrating the explanatory value of such intentional states, Eliminative Computationalism "accounts for" the PAs by arguing for their elimination—by attributing to them a mythical status as the theoretical posits of a rejected theory. Churchland adopts this eliminativist strategy, in a somewhat more naturalistic form, in his eliminativist materialism, to which we now turn.

In discussing the form of Eliminative Materialism developed by Churchland, I will first offer an account of his argument for the theoretical nature of the folk psychology in which he, like Stich, argues that the PAs figure as theoretical entities. I will then recount Churchland's arguments for the falsity of this folk psychology and for the attendant lack of empirical support it can lend to claims for the existence of the PAs. Finally, I will sketch the vision of a psychology and of a commonsense reconstructed on a neuroscientific foundation, devoid of intentional language, which Churchland envisions as a successor conceptual scheme.

Churchland (1979, 1981) offers what I construe as four distinct arguments for the status of our commonsense mentalistic framework—which he, with Stich, pejoratively labels "folk psychology"—as a scientific theory, subject to the same canons of epistemological evaluation as any other scientific theory. These are an argument from its use in the explanation of behavior, its use in the solution of the problem of other minds, the fact that the PA terms can most profitably be construed as adverbial expressions with slots for parameters, and the existence of a network of "laws of folk psychology."

Here is a succinct version of the argument from the use that the folk theory gets put to in the explanation and prediction of behavior:

> The fact is that the average person is able to explain, and even predict, the behavior of other persons with a facility and success that is remarkable. Such explanations standardly make reference to the desires, beliefs, fears, intentions, perceptions, and so forth, to which the agents are presumed subject.... Each of us understands others, as well as we do, because we share a tacit command of an integrated body of lore concerning the lawlike relations holding among external circumstances, internal states, and overt behavior. Given its nature and functions, this body of lore may quite aptly be called "folk psychology."
>
> This approach entails that the semantics of the terms in our familiar mentalistic vocabulary is to be understood in the same manner as the semantics of theoretical terms generally: the meaning of any theoretical terms is fixed or constituted by the network of laws in which it figures. (Churchland 1981, pp. 68–69)

This argument, is, of course, reminiscent of that found in Sellars 1956, and much of Churchland's position bears a marked Sellarsian stamp. The idea, fleshed out a bit, is that we are confronted by the need to explain and predict the observable behavior of our fellows. In order to do so, we, with some success, posit the existence of internal, unobservable phenomena, which we construct on the analogy of overt linguistic episodes (hence the parallelisms to the verbs of saying noted in the discussion of Methodological Solipsism above). These phenomena are then used in the prediction and explanation of behavior. The success we enjoy in employing these posits justifies our confidence in their existence. But what is important to note here—and what is easy to miss, given our current tendency to believe (falsely) that we directly introspect these phenomena in ourselves—is that our motivation for positing these phenomena and our reasons for confidence in their existence are epistemologically exactly on a par with our motivation for positing and our confidence in the existence of the theoretical entities of any science. As unobservable explanatory entities, the phenomena of folk psychology, including the PAs, must be treated as part of the scientific enterprise, and must be judged according to its standards.

Moreover, the semantics of PA expressions are therefore also hostage to the success or failure of the theory in which they are, on this account, embedded. We are hence not free to explicate the meanings of such expressions by any philosophical analysis independent of a consideration of the scientific status of folk psychology and of the place of these phenomena within the context of the scientific enterprise of psychology. This argument is the most fundamental of Churchland's four arguments, and contains the germs of the other three. For the account of the explanation of behavior is the foundation for the solution to the problem of other minds; the account resolves into the claim that there is a "network of laws" comprised by our common psychological folklore; and, as we shall see, the unpacking of the account of the use of the overt speech model in the characterization of inner episodes will yield Churchland's account of commonsense psychological predicates.

Churchland argues that by understanding the status of commonsense psychological predicates as theoretical terms he provides a natural solution to the problem of other minds, for if psychological phenomena are theoretical entities that provide our best explanation of our fellows' behavior, then there is no suggestion that we are performing a fallacious deductive inference from behavior to internal processes, or that we are arguing by analogy from our own case. Rather, we are simply performing an inference to the best explanation, exploiting the best theory we have of the behavior of humans.

The third argument Churchland adduces in favor of treating folk psychology as a theory is that it provides a straightforward and unproblematic analysis of what it is to have a PA in a way that demystifies the intentionality of PAs. If, he argues, we construe such expressions as "believes that" as theoretical terms, then we can understand them not as expressing relations between believers and propositions, or as expressions referring to states "containing" (in some difficult-to-specify sense) intentional inexistents, but rather as theoretical terms of the same category as such expressions as "has a mass of" and "has a velocity of." On this account, the embedded content clause of a PA ascription functions as a parameter that the theoretical term represented by the attitude verb takes as an argument, just as the numerical units of mass and velocity function as arguments to the theoretical terms of physics.

When the PAs are understood in this way, we see that the relations between the PAs are, as Fodor and Pylyshyn argued, relations held by the theory to obtain in virtue of their content. A final argument in favor of construing folk psychology as a theory depends upon Churchland's (1981, p. 71) claim that these relationships are cast as laws:

> ... the relations between the resulting PAs are characteristically the relations that hold between the propositions "contained" in them, relations such as entailment, equivalence, and mutual inconsistency.... All this permits the expression of generalizations concerning the lawlike relations that hold among PAs. Such laws involve quantification over propositions, and they exploit various relations holding in that domain. Thus, for example,
>
> $(x)(p)[(x \text{ fears that } p) \supset (x \text{ desires that } \sim p)]$
> $(x)(p)(q)[((x \text{ believes that } p) \&$
> $(x \text{ believes that (if } p \text{ then } q))) \supset$
> (barring confusion, distraction, etc. . . . ,
> $x \text{ believes that } q)]$

A curious feature of these laws, and of the conditions of PA ascription that Churchland notes, is that—although these generalizations are cast in an empirical, declarative form, similar to that of any natural law—buried in the attribution conditions of the PA predicates and in the motivation for asserting these laws is a critical normative component. We assert that whoever believes p and that $p \supset q$ also believes q not because we have overwhelming empirical evidence for the claim, but because whoever holds the first two beliefs *ought* to hold the third as well, and if he didn't for sufficiently many (or sufficiently obvious) instances of such triads we would begin to withhold belief ascriptions to him. This withholding would, again, have to do not with our view that our commonsense psychology is false, but rather with the view that our candidate believer fails in rationality— and this failure consists not in his violation of natural law but in his violation of epistemological *norms*. In this way, folk psychology, says Churchland, is infected with normative epistemology.

One might be led by this observation (as I am; see chapter 6) to urge that folk psychology is not really a scientific theory after all but is, rather, a portion of the manifest image subject to different epistemological strictures from scientific theories. But Churchland resists this temptation, arguing instead that part of the empirical content of folk psychology—and a respect, as we shall see, in which it is incorrect—is that actual persons mirror the generalizations suggested by normative epistemology. Hence, normative infection of an allegedly empirical theory is doubly pernicious—it calls into question the empirical content of the theory, and, to the extent that the normative assertions can be made descriptive, they are false.

There is one further line of argument against the theoretical nature of folk psychology that Churchland is concerned to dispose of, and that is the argument that our PA states are given to us directly, as the intentional states they are, in introspection:

> It has been claimed that the construal of our ordinary psychological concepts as theoretical concepts founders.... For in one's own case, of course, one generally ascribes [PAs] to oneself non-inferentially or observationally. One is a direct spectator of one's own mental life in a way that one is not a spectator of anyone else's. How then, the objection concludes, can we represent these *introspectively* applied concepts as *theoretical* concepts?
>
> With this objection we encounter ... the prejudice ... that a concept applicable in observation is *ipso facto* not a theoretical concept. We need only remind ourselves that observationality is a matter of a concept's mode of singular application, whereas theoreticity is a matter of its being semantically embedded in a framework of speculative assumptions, and the felt tension will disappear. For there is nothing inconsistent in the idea that one should be able to make reliable non-inferential applications of a concept whose semantic identity is fixed by a theory. All one needs to do is contrive a reliable habit of conceptual response to situations where the concept at issue truly applies. For ... such is the nature of observation judgments generally. Insofar as introspective judgments are just a species of observation judgment then, there is no problem at all about the theoretical nature of the concepts they characteristically involve. (Churchland 1979, pp. 95–96)

This is, of course, a restatement of the moral of the myth of Jones (Sellars 1956). The first-person judgment that one believes that *p* is not an incorrigible response to an episode "given" to consciousness as "that *p*" in character. Rather, it requires first having the concept (deriving originally from the concepts pertaining to overt saying) of an object with content, understanding *p*, and having mastered the theoretical vocabulary of commonsense psychology in which terms like "belief" are embedded to such a degree that one can reliably (though—as we have come to believe at least since Freud—not infallibly) apply that vocabulary to unobservable phenomena as one does the other, typically theory-laden terms of one's observation vocabulary.

Given these arguments in favor of construing commonsense psychology as constituting a scientific theory, Churchland is prepared to offer a number of arguments for its falsity; for replacing it, along with its ontology of PAs, with a neuroscientific theory of human and animal cognition and behavior, couched entirely in a nonintentional vocabulary; and hence for claiming that there is no such thing as a PA. He offers three related arguments: the argument from explanatory impotence, the argument from developmental and phylogenetic continuity, and the argument from theoretical incongruity. I will sketch each in turn.

The argument from explanatory impotence is not so much an argument as it is a litany of the failures to date of folk psychology (or any intentional psychology) to develop satisfying explanations of a wide range of phenomena that seem to fall squarely within the domain of psychology. Examples of these for Churchland are mental illness, spatial representation in vision, sleep, learning, and the emotions. The suggestion is that any theory with so very little to say about such central processes in its domain is shirking its explanatory duty and must be rated a very strong candidate for dismissal in favor of an explanatorily more powerful successor. (See Churchland 1981, pp. 74–75; Churchland 1979, pp. 114–115.) Furthermore, Churchland notes, all the lawlike generalizations of folk psychology are both hopelessly shallow and literally false as universal generalizations over fallible humans. We err; we act irrationally; we are not logically omniscient.

The argument from ontogenetic and phylogenetic continuity hinges upon the commitment of any psychology that counts among its theoretical posits intentional states with propositions or sentences as their contents, such as the PAs, to the linguistic or quasi-linguistic character of psychological processes and representations. Inasmuch as the neurophysiological and behavioral continua represented both by intraspecific human development and by the development of increasingly psychologically complex species is gradual and continuous, argues Churchland, any psychological theory of humans at early developmental stages, and of infrahumans, should be continuous with a good psychological theory of adult humans. But, he continues, in virtue of the dependence of a psychology committed to PAs on the ability of the organisms to which it applies to process sentences or sentence-like entities, and to satisfy canons of normative epistemology, this theoretical continuity is inaccessible to such a psychology. For very young humans and infrahumans fail to satisfy these conditions. They are not plausibly describable as representing propositions, since they have no language in which to represent them and since they are typically insufficiently rational to satisfy the set of laws in which the PA predicates get their sense. (See Churchland 1979, pp. 127–142.)

Finally, Churchland contends that these dimensions of explanatory failure are matched by an inability of intentional psychology to mesh with the more promising and better-entrenched theories couched in the language of neuroscience:

> ... If we approach *Homo sapiens* from the perspective of natural history and the physical sciences, we can tell a coherent story of his constitution, development, and behavioral capacities which encompasses particle physics, atomic and molecular theory, organic chemistry, evolutionary theory, biology, physiology, and materialistic neuroscience. That story, though still radically incomplete, is already extremely powerful, outperforming folk psychology at many points even in its own domain. And it is deliberately and self-consciously coherent with the rest of our developing world picture. In short, the greatest theoretical synthesis in the history of the human race is currently in our hands, and parts of it already provide searching descriptions and explanations of human sensory input, neural activity, and motor control.
>
> But folk psychology is no part of this growing synthesis. Its intentional categories stand magnificently alone, without visible prospect of reduction to that larger corpus.... Folk psychology suffers explanatory failures on an epic scale, ... it has been stagnant for at least twenty-five centuries, and ... its categories appear (so far) to be incommensurable with or orthogonal to the categories of the background physical science whose long-term claim to explain human behavior seems undeniable. Any theory which meets this description must be allowed a serious candidate for outright elimination. (Churchland 1981, pp. 74–75)

This argument, like the first and unlike the second, is not a principled argument against the possibility of an intentional psychology, but is rather a plausibility argument resting on the failure (to date) of the intentional categories of cognitive psychology to harmonize nicely with the physicalistic categories of the more fundamental physical sciences and on some strong presuppositions about the unity of science. Leaving aside the question of the adequacy of this set of arguments against any psychology cast in an intentional idiom, and hence against any psychology positing states like the PAs, let us turn to Churchland's alternative vision and see what replaces these phenomena in Eliminative Materialism.

The psychology envisioned by Eliminative Materialism is one whose categories and methods are those of neuroscience. The vocabulary of psychological theory would refer to neurotransmitter concentrations, firing frequencies and amplitudes of neurons, and so on. None of these phenomena, on this account, are identified by anything like their content, their "syntactic" structure, or even their "functional role" in the internal economy of the organism. All these predicates have strictly biological applicability conditions, and all generalizations of such a psychology will be straightforwardly neurophysiological. This eliminativism is hence far more radical than even that of Eliminative Computationalism.

Such a neuroscientific psychology would, Churchland argues, meet all three of his objections to intentionalistic psychology: Its explanatory power would be greater, in virtue of its finer grain, its ability to draw upon the explanatory resources of the more fundamental biological and physical sciences, and its ability to cope with psychological phenomena that resist propositional characterization (such as moods, mental illness, and sleep). One might, at this point, raise the objection implicit in such approaches as Methodological Solipsism and Naturalistic Individualism, viz., that while the explanations that such a psychology could provide would be in *some* sense more complete in virtue of their fine grain and reductive nature, there is a sense in which they would always fail to explain psychological phenomena *as psychological*—that they would miss generalizations that apply in virtue of the contents of these phenomena. (We saw such arguments not only earlier in this chapter but also in chapter 3.) This objection, at this point, however, would beg the question against Churchland, who, in virtue of the eliminativist stance his arguments are meant to establish, denies that there are any such psychological phenomena to explain, and that the proper phenomena in the purview of a scientific psychology just are the neurophysiological phenomena to which the generalizations he is after do apply. (To be sure, there is something distinctly odd about characterizing Churchland—who denies that there are such things as assertion and denial—as denying that there are such phenomena; however, I see no real alternative to this characterization.)

The other two objections to intentional psychology are also easily met by Eliminative Materialism. It is clearly congruent, in Churchland's sense, with the more fundamental physical and biological sciences, since such a psychology would, for all practical purposes, be identical with one of them—to wit, neuroscience. And in virtue of this neuroscientific cast, it is easy to see that such a psychology would exhibit the phylogenetic and ontogenetic continuity that Churchland sees as a desideratum.

But what, on this account, would happen to the world of commonsense psychology—to our experience, in everyday introspective and interactive awareness, of our own and others' psychological states? The picture painted here by Eliminative Materialism is even more radical. Recall Churchland's account of our commonsense psychological categories as theoretical terms. On this account, if the theory in which they are embedded and from which they derive their sense—intentional psychology—should be shed, as the foregoing argument suggests that it will, these theoretical terms will go the way of "phlogiston," "caloric fluid," and "yellow bile." They will drop from our vocabulary to be replaced with new introspective and third-person attributive psychological categories derived from the new neuropsychology. Just as we learned to introspect noninferentially and to attribute such (pseudo-)states as *believing that snow is white* and *desiring a sloop*, we will come to introspect noninferentially and attribute such states as *spikes of amplitude x* and *frequency y on tract z*, or something like that. In such a revised conceptual scheme, the manifest image of man-in-the-world and the scientific image would be one. Again, there would, on this account, be no loss of genuine phenomena or levels of description. All that would be lost would have been illusory or mythological in the first place.

Before we leave this account of Eliminative Materialism, a few words are necessary concerning why I take it to be, at least to some degree, a naturalistic version of eliminativism. Recall the distinction, with which we are operating, between naturalistic and solipsistic methodologies with respect to the individuation of psychological phenomena: Solipsistic approaches, such as Methodological Solipsism and Eliminative Computationalism, identify such phenomena solely in virtue of their interactions with other internal phenomena, without regard to any interactions of the organism with its environment and without any need to interpret any of these phenomena as referring to any real external objects, states of affairs, or properties. Naturalistic approaches, on the other hand, such as Naturalistic Individualism, identify such phenomena at least in part by noting the connections between internal phenomena and phenomena external to the organism, and hence often characterize psychological phenomena in terms of representational function.

On the face of it, given this way of drawing the distinction, Eliminative Materialism might seem to fall squarely in the solipsistic camp; if psychological phenomena are identified with neurological phenomena, it would seem clear that the criteria for individuating such phenomena would make reference only to internal states and processes of the organism. My reason for classifying this position (at least as it is developed by Churchland) as naturalistic, however, derives from two considerations: the fundamentally epistemological nature of the dichotomy at issue and the account of perceptual processes envisioned by Churchland.

In his discussion of perception, Churchland (1979, pp. 25–45) argues that in a post–Eliminative Materialism culture we will identify our sensory states not as sensations (say, *red*), and not necessarily in terms of their neurophysiological substrates, but perhaps for many purposes (e.g., epistemological, in order to give useful information about the external world, or for the purposes of interspecific comparisons in a general theory of the psychology of perception) as, e.g., *a sensation of incoming electromag-*

netic radiation of wavelength 0.5 × 10⁻⁶ *meters.* Such a description would be possible, given our expanded knowledge of the psychophysics of perception and our attendant ability to report noninferentially in appropriate language the distal causes of our perceptual states. But, more importantly, such a description would be scientifically appropriate if, for instance, we were classifying our perceptual responses to a particular class of stimuli and those of, say, dogs, for the purposes of a general account of mammalian perception, or if we just wanted to tell someone what color the wall is. Such an individuative scheme is, however, thoroughly naturalistic, despite its harmony with the neuropsychological framework Churchland envisions. It is for this reason—because Eliminative Materialism pushes its congruence with the physical sciences to the extent of aspiring to a congruence with the sciences of environment-organism interactions, and envisions encompassing these interactions in the purview of psychology, in a way foreign to approaches such as Methodological Solipsism and Eliminative Computationalism—that it is fair to classify it as naturalistic. (A further reason has to do with the epistemological consequences Churchland [1979, pp. 142–151] draws from Eliminative Materialism, viz., that Eliminative Materialism provides a foundation for a thoroughly naturalized, neurobiologically and ecologically grounded epistemology capable of characterizing and explaining the acquisition and representation of a sort of nonpropositional knowledge, but that is beyond the scope of this discussion.)

This completes our survey of the principal approaches to the problem of providing an explanation of the propositional attitudes in cognitive psychology. Before proceeding to examine these approaches critically with a view toward constructing a more viable alternative account, I want to review the state of play thus far.

The PAs pose a *prima facie* ontological and methodological problem for cognitive psychology. On the one hand, there are powerful reasons for thinking that many of the generalizations that would be of interest to psychology should be couched in terms of content. Indeed, this insight seems to lie at the very foundation of the functionalist philosophy of mind that undergirds the computational paradigm. Given the possibility of multiple, physically diverse instantiations of information-processing systems and the view that the correct level of description at which to characterize human psychological processes *qua psychological* is the IPS level, and given that the characterization of the states of an IPS are intentional, it seems to follow that the generalizations of interest to a cognitive psychology will be cast in intentional language. The overpowering intuition that our actions are often to be explained by our beliefs, knowledge, and other PAs lends credence to this view. On the other hand, there are powerful reasons for doubting that the PAs or other intentionally characterized states can figure in the ontology of a scientific psychology. The characterization of states as PAs appears to require attention to context, and hence to violate the autonomy principle, which has important independent motivation as a regulative methodological principle of psychological theory. Content ascriptions appear to be vague, to characterize states by similarity relations, and to depend upon the idiosyncratic perspective of ascribers. Intentional predicates have historically resisted attempts to embed them in a unified system of natural science. These countervailing considerations pose the central problem: Are the intentional predicates of our commonsense psychology—the categories of persons in the manifest image—explicable by or refinable into theoretical terms of scientific psychology, or must they be jettisoned by any such science in favor of more autonomous, precise, and projectible cognitive properties? And if the latter, what becomes of any claim to their reality?

Attempts to resolve this problem can be divided into four classes by two cross-cutting distinctions. *Reconciliationist* positions attempt to demonstrate the usefulness of intentional predicates, and the reality of the PAs in cognitive science; *eliminativist* positions attempt to demonstrate the inevitability of the demise of this class of predicates as theoretical terms, and the attendant unreality of the phenomena to which they purport to refer. *Solipsistic* positions attempt to characterize psychological phenomena solely by reference to evidence pertaining to the internal states and processes of the organism, and the relations these states and processes bear to one another, without recourse to information about the causal or semantic relations (if any) between these phenomena and anything in the organism's history or environment; *naturalistic* approaches allow the relevance of evidence gleaned from the observation of the organism's interaction with its environment in the characterization of its psychological states and processes, and allow their characterization, in the first instance, as relational, as connected essentially with extra-organismic phenomena (though it must be born in mind that this epistemological and methodological naturalism does not *straightforwardly* entail a nonindividualist ontology of the mental.

The remainder of this book will be devoted to demonstrating the untenability of each of these four approaches to solving the problem posed by the PAs, and to proposing an alternative analysis of the PAs and of psychological phenomena generally and a correspondingly different picture of the future of cognitive psychology and its relation to the other sciences. The next two chapters will be devoted to a critical examination of the reconciliationist and the eliminativist positions, respectively. I will argue that both reconciliationist positions presuppose an untenable individualistic theory of meaning and of the nature of psychological phenomena, and that the eliminativist positions miss the critical role of the central categories of the manifest image in grounding the scientific enterprise and in defining the domain of psychology. In chapter 7 I will develop my own accounts of the nature of psychological phenomena and psychological theory, arguing for a relational construal of psychological phenomena and for a naturalistic, intentional version of psychology, congruent with the other social sciences but perhaps less directly so with the physical and biological sciences, though retaining important theoretical relations to them.

Chapter 5
The Impossibility of Reconciliation

In this chapter I will argue that neither Methodological Solipsism nor Naturalistic Individualism can succeed, and that the reasons for their failure suggest not only that these two most obvious strategies for reconciling the computational theory of mind with a realistic commitment to the propositional attitudes must fail but that any reconciliation is impossible—that either the PAs or computationalism must go. I will begin by characterizing what I will call an Individualistic Theory of Meaning. I will argue that the truth of some such Individualistic Theory of Meaning is a necessary condition of the success of reconciliationism. As a preliminary to the more general argument that will follow, I will demonstrate that the arguments Pylyshyn marshals in support of Naturalistic Individualism are sufficient to demonstrate the untenability of Methodological Solipsism, and hence that Naturalistic Individualism is the only viable contender in the reconciliationist field. Subsequent argument will hence be directed against Naturalistic Individualism. The remainder of the discussion will be devoted to demonstrating first that Naturalistic Individualism, perhaps contrary to appearances, is committed to the Individualistic Theory of Meaning, and then to demonstrating the impossibility of any Individualistic Theory of Meaning. This discussion will set the stage for the discussion in the subsequent chapter of the possibility of the elimination of the PAs from the domain of psychology.

An Individualistic Theory of Meaning is not so much a theory of meaning as a theory of the ontology of meaningful phenomena. For our purposes, the phenomena at issue are the PAs, but we shall also want to bear in mind other intentional phenomena, such as overt linguistic tokens, both spoken and written. Burge (1982, p. 99) succinctly characterizes an Individualistic Theory of Meaning as involving "the view that mental states and processes individuated by [PA] expressions can be understood (or 'accounted for') purely in terms of non-intentional characterizations of the *individual subject's* acts, skills, dispositions, physical states, 'functional states,' and the effects of environmental stimuli on him, without regard to the nature of his physical environment or the activities of his fellows."

(Burge refers to this position as "individualism," as do I [1983] and Stillings et al. [1987]. I use "Individualistic Theory of Meaning" in this discussion to refer to such theories in order to emphasize both that the phenomena with which we are concerned are intentional and that the root of the problem with individualism lies in the intentionality of these phenomena.) Several features of this account deserve emphasis: the ontological rather than epistemological character of the position; the commitment of the position to the possibility of the redescription of the intentional in terms of the nonintentional (but in our case functional); and, most importantly, the commitment of the position to restricting the supervenience base of psychological phenomena to the set of nonpsychological phenomena occurring within the skin of the organism, perhaps even to those occurring within the organism's central nervous system. Before we embark on any criticism of the theory or any discussion of its relation to the computational paradigm or reconciliationism, it is essential to clarify each of these features of the account.

It is easy to mistake the Individualistic Theory of Meaning for an epistemological theory about the evidence we need to marshal in order to attribute a PA to a subject. Such an epistemological cousin might hold that the only evidence directly relevant in attributing a PA to an individual is information about the individual's nonintentional states, dispositions, etc., without regard to any relations that individual might bear to the putative objects of his PAs or to any other objects or persons external to him. This epistemological individualism might comprise views asserting that neurological evidence would suffice, that information about behavioral dispositions would suffice, that a computational characterization of the architecture and the current state of the system would suffice, and no doubt other views. This epistemological individualism, whether true or false, is distinct from and (at least *prima facie*) independent of the ontological individualism that is central to the Individualistic Theory of Meaning.

The important feature of the Individualistic Theory of Meaning is its commitment to the view that, regardless of the evidence necessary in order to justify a claim about the existence or occurrence of a particular psychological state or event such as a PA, the state or event itself depends for its character *qua* psychological (that is, *qua* representational) upon nothing but the nonrepresentational and nonrelational (that is, where "relational" means *relations to phenomena external to the subject of the PA*) states of the organism. Another way of putting this claim, which is reminiscent of Stich's replacement argument, is this: Varying the history and surroundings of the subject of a PA while holding its internal physical states and processes constant has no effect on its psychological states, events, or processes, including the scientifically correct characterization of its PAs in representational language. (Contrast this with the nonindividualistic character of such properties as *is owed ten dollars, knows that it is 2:00,* or *is the brother of John Smith,* which clearly depend upon the relations of their bearers to their environments.)

In light of this discussion, the independence of the ontological claim with which we shall be concerned from its epistemological cousin should be clear. One could, for instance, be ontologically individualistic but argue that the causal propensities of psychological phenomena are such that their character reveals itself only in a broad naturalistic context, and hence that the data necessary to discriminate one belief from another are always relational. Or one could imagine arguing that, though the PAs supervene on relational states of their bearers, they leave telltale individualistic "signatures" that enable one to tell with great reliability what PA a subject is in from individualistic data about that subject alone. At this stage, I am taking no position on whether the arguments or positions I have just imagined could ultimately succeed, or whether they are, on careful analysis, coherent. I will, in fact, argue shortly that the very considerations that drive one toward an epistemological naturalism entail an ontologically naturalistic (that is, nonindividualistic) position as well, at least with regard to the characterization of representational phenomena.

It is at least highly plausible that any Individualistic Theory of Meaning must be committed to the characterizability of any intentional state or process in terms of states or processes that are nonintentional. For a traditional (though not noncontroversial) hallmark of intentional phenomena is their object-directedness, and to be directed upon an object in this sense is generally thought to be related to it in some way. However, for a theory to be ontologically individualistic is for it to be committed to the claim that all psychological phenomena supervene only upon *non-relational* and hence nonintentional states of the organism. Thus, each and every intentional event or state is, on such an account, identifiable with some nonintentional event or state.

Now, this immediately raises a *prima facie* problem for reconciliationism, which must receive at least a plausible reply at this stage. As we have seen, the functionalist theory of mind, which underlies computational cognitive psychology, characterizes psychological phenomena under descriptions that involve interpreting those events, states, and processes at least as tokens of an abstract formal system—namely, the IPS that is taken to be represented by the underlying processes in the central nervous system of the organism that is the subject of those events, states, or processes. But this initial interpretation of the underlying neural processes as information processes already appears to involve the attribution of content to the phenomena posited by the psychological theory, where the content is described in the vocabulary of the IPS represented by the central nervous system of the organism. Hence, it appears that no computational model of an intentional phenomenon can involve the redescription of the intentional in terms of the nonintentional, but rather that all such theories involve the redescription of the intentional in terms of more fundamental intentional categories.

If this line of reasoning were correct, then, it would appear that the Individualistic Theory of Meaning would be *trivially* incompatible with functionalism, and that reconciliationism, if committed to the Individualistic Theory of Meaning, would hence be a hopeless nonstarter. In fact, I will argue below that something like this line of reasoning is correct, but the argument must be a bit subtler. For now, it is important to note that, whatever the problems with the Individualistic Theory of Meaning, to view it as undermining the functionalist enterprise in this straightforward way would be erroneous. There are two ways of putting this point. First, it is important to note that, on the functional model just sketched, even if the phenomena in terms of which PAs are analyzed in the first instance are characterized as intentional, in virtue of being characterized as information-processing states, they in turn are identified with the physical states and processes of the nervous system that underlie them. The analysis is hence, when complete, thoroughly individualistic in this sense. Second, as a consequence of this first observation, it can be seen that, on this model, the characterization of these states as information-processing states rather than as physiological states is a matter of epistemological convenience, not one of ontological import. Their ostensibly intentional character vanishes once one realizes that their character as states and processes of an IPS is no more than a convenient shorthand for their physiological character. We will return to this point in chapters 7 and 8; see also Dennett 1975 and Haugeland 1978.

The most important feature of an Individualistic Theory of Meaning is its commitment to a narrow supervenience base for all psychological phenomena. This point has emerged implicitly in the foregoing discussion, but it deserves emphasis. An Individualistic Theory of Meaning is committed to the view that no two individuals could differ psychologically without differing in some individualistic physical respect as well. Put another way, according to an Individualistic Theory of Meaning, psychological events, states, and processes are supervenient upon individualistic physical events, states, and processes. (For discussions of varieties of supervenience, see Garfield 1983; Haugeland 1982; Hellman and Thompson 1975, 1976; and Kim 1978, 1982, 1984a, 1984b.)

This completes our sketch of the principal commitments of an Individualistic Theory of Meaning. Such a theory is committed to the thesis that meaningful phenomena can be identified with the discrete, spatiotemporally isolated tokens of nonintentional objects that, in some intuitive sense, express them, such as ink marks or neural processes, without regard to the relations obtaining between these nonintentional objects and their environments or contexts. We can now proceed to discuss the reasons for its centrality to the reconciliationist enterprise, before launching an attack on the enterprise that has as its target the Individualistic Theory of Meaning itself.

Recall the two positions reconciliationism is meant to reconcile. The first is the computationalist, functionalist model of mind that underlies much current research in cognitive psychology and much of the philosophy of mind inspired thereby. The version of functionalism on the table, as I suggested in chapter 2, is representational functionalism. But even this liberal account of the nature of the relation of psychological phenomena to the physical or biological phenomena upon which they supervene—interpolating, as it does, a number of levels of description between the two—is committed to the token identification of particular psychological events, states, and processes with particular computational events, states, and processes, and these in turn with particular physical events, states, and processes. (See Lycan 1981; Pylyshyn 1984, pp. 32–33.) Without this commitment, the notion of the mind as an IPS would be hollow. For, as we have seen, an IPS just is a physically instantiated system each of whose physical states and processes can be interpreted as an information-processing state or process.

The position with which the representational functionalism embodied by the IPS model of the mind is to be reconciled is a realistic commitment to the PAs as theoretical entities within the domain of psychology. This commitment involves not only the claim that they are legitimate explananda for such a psychology, but also that they are states in which the human IPS is capable of being, that they are representations over which its information processes are defined, and that the PA locutions form predicates that figure in the characterization of the psychological events posited in theoretical explanations of human cognitive capacities.

With these two positions in view, it should be clear that their compatibility entails the truth of the Individualistic Theory of Meaning. For the IPS model of the mind entails functionalism, which in turn entails a token-identity relation between psychological and physical phenomena. By itself, this does not require an individualistic interpretation of the PAs, and hence it does not entail the truth of an Individualistic Theory of Meaning. For one could deny, as eliminativists do, the possibility of states such as the PAs figuring in an articulated psychology. But if the PAs are to be counted among the phenomena posited on a realistic interpretation of a psychological theory, then they must be identified with particular tokens of physically—i.e., individualistically—characterized states of the organism. Failure to identify them in this way would be to jettison the commitment to the token-identity relation between psychological and neurobiological phenomena, and hence to functionalism and the IPS model of psychological explanation. But, as the Individualistic Theory of Meaning was characterized in the preceding discussion, this commitment to an individualistic identification of token PAs with token physical states just is a commitment to the truth of that theory of the ontological status of meaningful phenomena.

Before undertaking the task of arguing in detail against the possibility of an Individualistic Theory of Meaning, and hence against the possibility of reconciliation, I want to note an anticipation of this strategy within the reconciliationist camp, in the form of an argument implicitly mobilized by Pylyshyn in defense of Naturalistic Individualism against Methodological Solipsism. We will hence step back and explore just why Naturalistic Individualism is able, at least for the moment, to secure the high ground against Methodological Solipsism, only to see that this advantage is only momentary. We will then turn to the attack on the Individualistic Theory of Meaning.

In chapter 4 we rehearsed a set of arguments in favor of Naturalistic Individualism as against Methodological Solipsism. Let us first call them very quickly to mind, and then consider the thread that runs through all of them, which we shall see is an implicit attack on the Individualistic Theory of Meaning as it is embodied by Methodological Solipsism.

The first of these arguments rested on Pylyshyn's claim that any explanation of behavior like Mary's running from the burning building in terms of initially uninterpreted formal symbols and symbol processing, such as that required by Methodological Solipsism, will be incomplete unless supplemented by an account of why *those* symbols were activated in the way that they were and why they were processed in the way that they were. And such an account would be an account of how those symbols came to have the representational character they do, which, on Naturalistic Individualism, would be an account of why they were caused by the stimuli that caused them, why they interact with other such symbols and symbolic processes as they do, and why they issue in the behavior to which they give rise.

The second argument rests on the claim that even to characterize a physical event, state, or process as computational in the first place (a move essential to any functionalist theory, including both Naturalistic Individualism and Methodological Solipsism) is to engage in interpretation, and on the claim that the only data that could possibly support the selection of the objects to interpret, and the interpretations assigned to them, include naturalistic data about the way the organism behaves and responds to stimulation.

Finally, we saw that the Naturalistic Individualist charges the Methodological Solipsist with a failure to sustain a realistic interpretation of psychological theory, in virtue of ignoring the actual connections between representations and their environmental objects in favor of an indeterminate set of mutually incompatible but equally vindicated possible interpretations of representational phenomena. This inability to sustain a psychological realism arose, according to Naturalistic Individualism, from the claim (central to Methodological Solipsism) that the actual relations of the organism to the environment are irrelevant to its psychological characterization, coupled with the availability of multiple equally sound interpretations for any isolated computational system.

There is a central theme running through these three arguments that makes it tempting to say that they are really three expressions of the same underlying argument: Any functionalist theory of mind must hold that the characterization of psychological phenomena *qua psychological* is an act of interpretation. The psychologist comes to the organism, on such an account, as the cryptanalyst comes to his enemy's coded message. But the data needed to fix a unique (or even a relatively most plausible) interpretation of the biological code extend well beyond the physical features of the code. It is, of course, just the same with the cryptanalyst. Without some hunches about the language being coded (e.g., Russian or FORTRAN) or the subject matter (e.g., honeybees or aircraft), there is no place to start. What is more, the psychobiological cryptanalyst has the additional task of determining which biological events, states, or processes are to be candidates for interpretation in the first place (e.g., seretonin concentrations, electrical waveforms, neural firings). If this code is to be cracked, the Naturalistic Individualist asserts, it will be done only through attending carefully to the interactions of the conjectured IPS with its environment and noting which events, states, and processes give rise to what kinds of behavior and which are caused by which stimulation, in order to identify the particles of the code and some of their possible significations. Methodological Solipsism, in its determined ignorance of these sources of data, gives up the possibility of vindicating any interpretation and so abandons the quest of a realistic account of a human IPS.

Naturalistic Individualism, on this view, takes these naturalistic facts seriously in arriving at a characterization of the architecture of the mind and of the psychological phenomena it supports, and does so while retaining its allegiance to a functionalist ontology. On Naturalistic Individualism, the phenomena of interest to psychology are characterized for the purposes of psychological theory by reference to their content, and the facts that fix their content are the connections between these phenomena and their environmental causes and effects. But at the same time, the argument goes, Naturalistic Individualism is not abandoning an individualistic psychology of the kind demanded by anyone who embraces the replacement argument or any of the principal motivating arguments for Methodological Solipsism (such as the arguments from the parallelism of verbs of saying and the PA verbs or the argument from the impossibility of naturalism). Although the facts responsible for determining interpretations are on this account naturalistic (comprising relations of the organism to distal stimuli and objects), the phenomena that get interpreted (only *internal* states and processes), and the generalizations over them, obey the individualistic supervenience principles of the Individualistic Theory of Meaning. The meaningful phenomena that are the theoretical entities of such a psychology are still, on this account, individualistic states and processes within individual organisms.

The arguments mounted against Methodological Solipsism by Naturalistic Individualism seem to me to be essentially sound, but the further positive moral drawn is, I will argue, untenable for reasons suggested by these critical arguments themselves. For what makes these arguments compelling is the underlying insight that essential to the characterization of the content of any representational state is its connection to its environment. Considered solipsistically, no state can be assigned representational character. But Naturalistic Individualism tries to have its cake and eat it too. Having established the essential role of naturalistic evidence in the interpretation of events or states as representational, the Naturalistic Individualist turns around and asserts that, despite the essential role that the nonindividualistic properties of these phenomena play in their individuation, their *nature*—their identity *qua* psychological phenomena of particular types—can be specified individualistically. It is this balancing act between epistemological naturalism and ontological individualism that makes Naturalistic Individualism so attractive. However, I will develop arguments suggesting that it is an impossible act, and that the very considerations that motivate epistemological naturalism can be brought to bear ontologically as well.

I will now build the case against any Individualistic Theory of Meaning, and hence ultimately against the possibility of reconciliation. I will begin by developing a set of arguments (which appear in various forms in Putnam 1975a, Burge 1979 and 1982, and Garfield 1983) to the effect that propositional attitudes cannot be characterized individualistically insofar as they are identified by their content. I will then present a preliminary sketch of an account of the ontological character of the PAs. Finally, I will discuss an argument of Putnam's (1981) that suggests that something like this sketch must be correct given the case against an individualistic theory of belief.

Putnam's classic (1975a) Twin-Earth example has been taken by many to show that Frege's triad of desiderata for the objects of PAs is unsatisfiable—

that nothing can be at the same time a determiner of extensions, a primary bearer of truth-value, and what the mind grasps (or, as Putnam [1975a, p. 227] puts it, "meanings just ain't in the *head*"). The further moral has been drawn (Garfield 1983; Burge 1979, 1982) that the contents of psychological states are determined not solely by the current individualistically characterized states of their bearers but also by certain features of their bearers' environments and linguistic communities. Here is a version of Putnam's example, as developed by Burge:

> ... we are to conceive of a near duplicate of our planet Earth, called "Twin Earth." Except for certain features about to be noted (and necessary consequences of these features), Twin-Earth duplicates Earth in every detail.... Many of the inhabitants of one planet have duplicate counterparts on the other, with duplicate macro-physical, experiential, and dispositional histories.
>
> One key difference between the two planets is that the liquid on Twin-Earth that runs in rivers and faucets and is called "water" by those who speak what is called "English" is not H_2O, but a different liquid with a radically different chemical formula XYZ.... In translating into English occurrences of "water" in the mouths of Twin-Earthians, we would do best to coin a new nonscientific word "twater"....
>
> A second key difference ... is that the scientific community on Earth has determined that the chemical structure of water is H_2O, whereas the scientific community on Twin-Earth knows that the structure of twater is XYZ. These pieces of knowledge have spread into the respective lay communities, but have not saturated them. In particular, there are numerous scattered individuals on Earth and Twin-Earth untouched by the scientific developments. It is these latter individuals who have duplicate counterparts.
>
> Now suppose that Adam is an English speaker and that $Adam_{te}$ is his counterpart on Twin-Earth. Neither knows the chemical properties of what he calls "water." ... We further suppose that both have the same qualitative perceptual intake and qualitative streams of consciousness, the same movements, the same behavioral dispositions and inner functional states (non-intentionally and individualistically described). (Burge 1982, pp. 100−101)

Now, suppose that Adam and $Adam_{te}$ each have the same attitude (say, belief) toward propositions which would be expressed homophonically in English and Twin-English. Suppose that Adam and $Adam_{te}$, in virtue of their thoroughgoing micro-similarity (waiving the presence of water or twater in their bodies), each have a belief which each expresses as "My goldfish needs to have his water changed." Adam's belief is about water;

Adam$_{te}$'s is about twater. A correct third-person belief attribution to Adam would be "Adam believes that his goldfish's water needs to be changed," while a correct belief attribution to Adam$_{te}$ would be "Adam$_{te}$ believes that his goldfish's twater needs to be changed." The homonymy of "water" in English and "water" in Twin-English cannot by itself issue in the identity of these psychological states, and to appeal to the individualistic similarities between Adam and his twin at this stage would beg the question. In fact, Adam, unless he has been reading some recent philosophy, has no beliefs whatever about twater, and Adam$_{te}$ has none about water. The two words mean quite different things, since they determine quite different extensions, and neither Adam nor Adam$_{te}$ has had any contact with anyone who knows what the counterpart to his "water" means or with anything in the extension of that counterpart word. (Parallel points can be made, without such elaborate thought experiments, using beliefs expressed by means of indexicals, such as "it is now 2:00 P.M.," which seem to involve attitudes toward different propositions when uttered at different times, despite the possible physical and functional identities of the subjects of those beliefs at different times. See Dennett 1982, Kaplan 1978 and Perry 1979.)

What are we to say about Adam and Adam$_{te}$? There is a clear sense in which may things about them are very similar, and there is a strong temptation to say that whatever about them can be relevant to a scientific psychology must be identical. After all, they are, *ex hypothesi*, identical structurally, computationally, and dispositionally. Nonetheless, there is an equally strong sense in which there are certain domains about which, despite this individualistic similarity within those domains, they share no PAs. An approach taken by Putnam (1975a) and by Fodor (1980), and in a slightly different form by Perry (1979), is to distinguish a subject's *narrow* psychological state from a *wide* psychological state, and then to argue (as do Fodor and Perry, but not Putnam) that only the narrow state can be a proper object for psychology. The narrow state, on this account, would be assigned and individuated by reference to a content which, for instance, would be neutral between *water* and *twater* (perhaps something like "clear, potable, wet stuff, which freezes at 0°C," etc.).

But this strategy can't work, for two reasons. First, no matter how hard one tries to specify a neutral "narrow" content for such psychological states as the PAs, each such proposed content will be subject to the same "Twin-Earthization" strategy applied to some term in the embedded clause used to characterize the attitude, if the content is specified in terms of a set of general predicates, as above. In Twin-English, "potable" might refer only to those liquids that have no carcinogenic potential whatever, whereas in our English it refers to any liquid with no short-term propensity to produce harm, or something like that. If, on the other hand, we avoid replacing "water" with some set of descriptors, and suggest that the content is to be picked out as *de re*, then Adam is clearly in relation to water and Adam$_{te}$ is clearly in the same relation to twater. (See Baker 1987 for another defense of this view that the "narrow content strategy" allows insufficient room for maneuvering.) Second, and underlying the first point, even such a narrow state would be sensitive to facts about the environment in which the subject of that state is embedded—particularly the linguistic environment, or, more specifically, the linguistic community that determines the meanings of the words used in characterizing the state in question. An example drawn from Burge 1979 brings this out nicely: Consider another counterfactual community, also inhabiting a planet just like our Earth in all respects save that in their Twin-English the word "arthritis" refers not only to arthritis but also to various painful inflammatory disorders of the bones not confined to the joints, including what we correctly refer to as "periostitis," in distinction to *arthritis*. Now, we can imagine Adam (still in his state of moderate scientific ignorance) suffering from arthritis, waking up one day with a sore thigh, and thinking to himself, "My arthritis is spreading to my thigh." He is of course (one might say *necessarily*, in the right Kripkean mood) wrong. But his twin, Adam$_{te2}$, who inhabits our new counterfactual community and who has the same adequate-for-everyday-purposes but rather vague and somewhat erroneous (though of course in different respects) concept of what is called on his world "arthritis" (let us call it "twarthritis"), in virtue of sharing the same individualistically characterized physical and functional state, thereby believes something true, namely that his twarthritis (which he would call, correctly, "arthritis") has spread to his thigh.

It is clear, just as it is in the Twin-Earth cases, that Adam and Adam$_{te2}$ differ in their wide psychological state—in their PA, as this would be ordinarily construed. Is there any way of capturing their narrow state (which, on the Fodorian strategy, ought to be the same, given their structural similarities) that does not result in this same divergence? Given that the linguistic meaning of "arthritis" is fixed in each world, and hence for each Adam, by the respective communities of experts on those worlds, and given that it is different for each Adam, the only locution that would seem appropriate to describe the content of either of their beliefs, viz., "My arthritis has spread to my thigh," picks out different narrow contents in the two cases (unless the individuation of contents proceeds along lines spelled out by the literal shapes of the words Adam and Adam$_{te2}$ are disposed to utter, in which case we lose the possibility of cross-language belief identification and we are back to square one).

Here is another way to put this point: The proponent of an individualistic theory of meaning must identify a level of semantic description of internal states intermediate between one that assigns broad contents and one that makes all attitudes *de expressione*. Broad content will not work for

the individualist, because at such a level of description the two Adams'
states diverge. *De expressione* will not work, because speakers of different
languages may share beliefs and because of the possibility of different but
homophonic beliefs in different (or the same) language(s). If there is such an
intermediate level of description, it must assign the same beliefs to the two
Adams. The only available option would seem to be the one in which the
contents of the beliefs were specified phenomenalistically, for any non-
phenomenalistic account falls prey to repeated Twin-Earthization. However
(and this is not the place to rehearse *these* hoary arguments), phenom-
enalism is a crazy theory of meaning. Hence, it is hard to see where there
is room for the kind of "content" the narrow-content theorists are after.

The moral of this case is—and, in this light, the moral of the original
Twin-Earth case can be seen to be—that the contents of any psychological
phenomenon individuated by content, such as a PA, depend not only upon
the individualistic properties of the subject of that state but also upon such
relational facts as the situation of that individual in his or her linguistic
community, the semantic conventions adopted by that community, and
that individual's relations to the objects of his or her attitudes.

A curious feature of individualist theorists is that they all seem to think
that there is something terribly special about the skin. Maybe this is the
legacy of behaviorism, but whatever its origin this prejudice deserves
examination. The pride of place given to central processes and the methodological antipathy toward ascribing psychological significance to motor
and sensory processes ought, one would think, to lead a consistent individualist to draw the boundaries of the psychological at the neuromuscular
synapse and the sensory receptor—that is, well within the skin. But, by
parity of reasoning, why accord psychological significance to mere efferent
motor impulses or afferent sensory impulses? Presumably only more central
processes are psychologically relevant. This kind of reasoning appears to
be unstoppable short of the pineal gland! Now of course a sane individualist will set about justifying a boundary somewhere short of nowhere—
maybe at the boundary of the nervous system, maybe at the first reasonably complex ganglionic structures, or maybe in the cerebral cortex. But,
although boundaries can be drawn, it is far from clear that nonarbitrary
ones can be.

Taking this conclusion seriously entails rejecting an individualist account
of the nature of PAs, for stories like Putnam's and Burge's show us that not
only does the evidence that we need in order to justify the ascription of a
PA to an individual go beyond any individualistic data about that individual, but *the fact that an individual is in a particular PA is a nonindividualistic
fact about that individual—that is, being in a PA is a matter of standing in a set
of relations to one's environment, including (at least in the case of the subjects of de
dicto PAs) one's linguistic community.* Thus far, this conclusion does not

express a wholesale rejection of the Individualistic Theory of Meaning. One might still assert that, although the PAs are in some sense special in their relational character, other meaningful phenomena might be characterizable individualistically. But this would be a mistake, and a detour through a brief discussion of the intentionality of language might help demystify the nonindividualistic account of the PAs I am developing and indicate its location in the broader enterprise of the philosophy of mind.

Besides psychological phenomena, the other obvious class of representational objects is that comprising strings of natural languages, written or spoken. I want to argue, in order to clarify the nature of the relational character of the PAs and in order to ground it, that that relational character is shared by linguistic tokens when they are considered as representational— that is, that such contentful linguistic items as assertions, statements, and questions supervene on broader bases than simply the ink marks or sound waves that appear to underlie them. When understood properly, this is not a surprising thesis; in fact, it is part and parcel of the account of meaning and meaningful phenomena that is the legacy of the later Wittgenstein and of Sellars. An appreciation of its ontological consequences, however, has been absent from much thinking about the foundations of cognitive science.

We have seen that an appreciation of the consequences of the Twin-Earth example and of related examples forces us to think of the ontological supervenience base of the PAs extending to whatever determines their contents, and that this can encompass much that is beyond the skin of the organism that is the nominal subject of the PA. That is, in attributing such a psychological state to an organism, we are attributing to that organism a location in a network of representational phenomena, and hence in a network of relations to its environment, rather than describing its internal condition. Now it should be apparent that, in ascribing content to a linguistic expression, we are engaged in a similar task.

Consider the familiar Sellarsian analysis of a statement such as "'Rot' means *red*" as having the logical form "'Rot' is a ·red·", which in turn is analyzed as "'Rot' plays the same role in its language that 'red' plays in ours". Such an analysis of the ascription of meaning to linguistic objects characterizes such ascriptions as locating their objects in a network of other linguistic objects, in a network of characteristic inference patterns—in short, in a network whose total function is to provide a representation of reality, a mechanism for drawing inferences within that representational scheme, and a set of language-entrance and language-exit transitions which hook the scheme up to perception and action. So, for 'rot' to be a ·red· is for it to be characteristically used to predicate redness of objects, for such predications to license the inference that those objects are not green, and so on.

A linguistic item, on this account of the ascription of meaning, is not a mere token of ink or vibrating larynx and air; it is, rather, such a thing in a conventionally constituted context. But what must be emphasized in this characterization is that the role of the context—the language and the linguistic community in which a linguistic token has its meaning—is not simply epistemological but is ontological as well. More straightforwardly, it is not simply that we need evidence about the behavioral and inferential role that a linguistic item plays in its linguistic context in order to interpret it, though to be sure we do, but rather that its meaning is constituted by that role, and hence that the supervenience base of a linguistic item *qua linguistic* must be taken to extend as broadly as the community of language users and conventions in which it is situated. The ontology and the meaning of words are hence no more susceptible of explication by an Individualistic Theory of Meaning than are the ontology and the meaning of representational psychological phenomena such as the PAs.

There are two reasons why, from this Sellarsian perspective, this should not be surprising. First, such a perspective involves an account of psychological events and states on which such events and states (at least those that are representational) are understood as tokens *in foro interno* of types that also comprise external linguistic tokens, so a belief that snow is white is a ·Snow is white·. The ontological nonindividualism of the PAs would thus emerge simply as a special case of their quasi-linguistic representational character, as I have argued that it must. The Individualistic Theory of Meaning is incorrect as a theory of meaningful objects quite generally, and only incidentally false of the PAs. The second reason for the failure of an Individualistic Theory of Meaning as an account of the PAs is equally interesting. There is a *prima facie* plausible pretheoretic distinction, embraced by Fodor (1978, 1979, 1980), between psychological states that are infected with normative and naturalistic characteristics (such as knowledge, which requires the truth and justification of its propositional object over and above the narrow state of its subject) and pure, narrow states (which carry no such naturalistic or normative presupposition). The hope of such reconciliationist theorists as Fodor and Pylyshyn is that the PAs can be characterized as normatively antiseptic states that—unlike knowledge, which obviously must receive naturalistic treatment—can be treated as narrow, individualistically characterized states. (Recall the discussion of Thomason's [1977] result in chapter 4 above.) What I now want to suggest is that a further way of understanding the relational character of the PAs is to see that they are, simply in virtue of their representational character, as normatively infected as knowledge. I will sketch the reasons for this view here, and will return to them in detail in chapter 7.

For the present, let us (as we have been doing implicitly throughout the preceding discussion) waive certain questions about the applicability of PA predicates to infralingual humans, animals, and machines, and concentrate on the implications of the application of these predicates to mature persons. In the next two chapters, the question of what (if any) differences there are between the PAs we attribute to less cognitively competent subjects of psychological theory and those we attribute to ourselves will be addressed at greater length. To attribute a PA, such as belief, to a subject is (not necessarily exhaustively) to attribute to him or her certain cognitive capacities, inferential and behavioral dispositions, the possession of certain concepts, and hence the possession of a certain amount of knowledge. Suppose that we assert that (0) John believes *that the blue whale is extinct*. It seems clear that any of the following assertions would be incompatible with that sincere belief ascription:

(1) John sincerely asserts that blue whales are plentiful.
(2) John has no idea what whales are, and does not possess the concept of extinction or that of a species.
(3) John infers that blue whales are extinct from the fact that grass is green, citing *modus ponens* to justify the inference, and deduces from the fact that they are extinct that they are capable of flight.

Asserting (1) would involve ascribing to John a behavioral disposition that seems, even given the falsity of any straightforwardly behavioristic account of belief, to be manifestly incompatible with the truth of (0). One might argue that this incompatibility is only apparent, and that a *de dicto* reading of (0) would be compatible with (1). But this would be a mistake, for the correct way to report the only belief that might be alluded to by a reading of (0) compatible with (1) would be (4) "John believes that the sentence 'Blue whales are extinct' expresses a truth, though he doesn't know what it means" (the *de expressione* reading of Cresswell [1985]). Such a sentence would be true, perhaps, if John was a monolingual Korean who heard someone he respects assert in English that blue whales are extinct, but then, if (1) were true of John, (0) would be a most misleading characterization of his cognitive state.

For similar reasons, (2) is incompatible with (0). It seems that if John has not even mastered the concepts that are central to the belief ascribed to him, there can simply be no sense to the ascription, except in the highly attenuated construal embodied by (4). I believe that the entailment by (0) of the falsity of anything like (2)—an entailment that follows from the fact that a believer is also necessarily a concept-mobilizer—is at the bottom of the epistemological impurity of the PAs. I will argue in chapter 7 that it is a necessary condition of having and mobilizing concepts that one have some knowledge regarding their conditions of applicability. Hence, I will argue that if knowledge is impure, so is belief.

Finally, (3) is incompatible with (0) for reasons that strike directly at the normative character, and hence the essential embeddedness in a community capable of enforcing norms, of the PAs. Asserting (3) calls into question the possibility of sustaining the interpretation of John's psychological states and processes as having the content they are asserted to have. If the interpretive scheme by means of which we characterize his IPS assigns him these bizarre inference patterns in a wholesale fashion, there is a strong sense in which it has to be wrong. If John's inferential behavior is sound globally and is bizarre only in this vicinity, that at least suggests that the interpretation of his psychological state as *about whales* is seriously questionable, for the assigning of content to psychological phenomena is a matter of interpretation, and the evidence that vindicates an interpretation can only be that the interpreted text comes out "making sense" (see Haugeland 1979, 1981b). If the text in question is a person's psychological history, then making sense amounts to believing mostly the truth, behaving mostly appropriately, perceiving mostly what is there, and performing mostly valid inferences (see Davidson 1970a, 1977). It involves forming beliefs and performing actions that are usually justified. This is wherein John would fail if (3) were warranted, and such failure would issue in the impossibility of justifying (0) as an interpretation of John's psychological state and perhaps in the impossibility of interpreting his psychological states or beliefs at all.

If this discussion of John is correct, we can make a further observation that strikes at the impossibility of an Individualistic Theory of Meaning and hence at the impossibility of reconciliation. In order for a subject of psychological states to have states interpretable as meaningful, that subject must consistently (though not, of course, perfectly) mobilize relevant concepts, justify its beliefs and actions, and, in short, know something about the subject matter that comprises the objects of its representational states. And, given the normative character of these epistemological capacities and their manifest failure to be accommodatable by an individualistic theory, it follows that even such apparently epistemologically antiseptic states as belief carry this naturalistic infection.

So far I have argued that, in order to reconcile a realistic interpretation of attributions of predicates that range over anything like our commonsense vocabulary of the PAs—that is, of predicates that classify psychological phenomena in virtue of their representational content—with the functionalist theory of mind that underlies much current computational psychology, one would have to adopt an Individualistic Theory of Meaning. This was because the classification of these phenomena as representational involves their classification as meaningful, and because their identification as functionally characterized states of individual organisms requires (as I argued in chapter 3) individualism. I have offered two sorts of arguments against the possibility of such a theory of meaningful phenomena. The first relies on

Twin-Earth examples, and generalizes their moral to an account of the social and environmental nature of the supervenience base of meaningful phenomena. The second, which I have only introduced but which I will discuss in more detail in chapter 7, relies upon the observation that, Fodor to the contrary, such psychological states as belief, and presumably all representational states, are bound up so tightly with such nonindividualistic states as knowledge that they cannot be attributed independently and so must partake of the same nonindividualistic treatment required for all normatively characterized states and processes. Before turning to some final observations about the location of the seeds of these arguments in Naturalistic Individualism, I want to discuss the way in which similar points emerge from Putnam's (1981) discussion of brains in a vat.

Putnam asks us to consider a case that, he argues, is physically (though, curiously, not metaphysically, or logically) possible: that we are not fully embodied inhabitants of an actual world comprising the objects and events that manifest themselves to us, but rather that we are all brains floating in a vat of nutrient fluid, with our nerves connected to computers which cause us to have experiences identical to those we would have were the world the way it appears to be. Putnam argues that this supposition is necessarily false:

> [On the assumption that we are brains in a vat] "vat" refers to vats in the image in vat-English, or something related (electronic impulses or program features), but certainly not to real vats, since the use of "vat" in vat-English has no causal connection to real vats.... Similarly, "nutrient fluid" refers to a liquid in the image in vat-English, or something related.... It follows that if their "possible world" is really the actual one, and we are really the brains in a vat, then what we now mean by "we are brains in a vat" is that *we are brains in a vat in the image* or something of that kind (if we mean anything at all). But part of the hypothesis that we are brains in a vat is that we aren't brains in a vat in the image (i.e., what we are "hallucinating" isn't that we are brains in a vat). So, if we are brains in a vat, then the sentence "We are brains in a vat" says something false (if it says anything). In short, if we are brains in a vat, then "We are brains in a vat" is false. So it is (necessarily) false. (Putnam 1981, p. 15)

Putnam mobilizes this argument against what he calls a "magical theory of reference," one that asserts that intrinsic features of representational states determine their reference (say, their resemblance to their referent, or something like that). But it can be wielded to make the more general point that I am after (and Putnam implicitly wields it in just this way): The meanings of any semantically primitive objects, whether these are external linguistic tokens or internal psychological tokens, and hence the meanings of any complex objects composed of them, depend essentially on two kinds of relational facts which stand in the way of any Individualistic Theory of Meaning: reference-inducing relations of referring expressions to their referents and (more generally) the set of conventions regarding linguistic use.

For an expression Ψ to refer to some referent Φ, there must, as Putnam argues, be some causal relation between Ψ and Φ in virtue of which tokens of Ψ can be used to refer to Φ. No intrinsic feature of Ψ could suffice to establish such relation. We need not endorse any specific account of the nature or natures of the relation or relations that are either necessary or sufficient to induce reference. It would suffice for the purpose of discrediting the Individualistic Theory of Meaning to note that there must be some such causal connection, and demonstrating this necessity was the burden of the first part of the discussion of the preceding section. But we can go further than this. In order for a relation to be reference-inducing, and hence to serve as part of the foundation for a semantic theory of a system of events, states, and processes such as an interpretation of a set of psychological processes and states as representational, the relation must be conventional and must be set in the context of a system of linguistic conventions. Thus, even if Ψ resembled Φ exactly, this fact would be neither necessary nor sufficient for Ψ's referring to Φ. Moreover, even if Φs were reliably to cause inscriptions of Ψ to be produced, this relation would not suffice to establish reference. Φs might be painful (perhaps the only painful stimuli in the environment of the Ψ-writers), and Ψ might be an expression of agony. In order for a referential relation to be established, there must be a convention among the users of Ψ to use it to refer to Φ. Anything less will not be sufficient.

At this point it might be argued that all this is plausible as an account of at least some of the necessary conditions of linguistic expressions functioning representationally, but that for internal psychological phenomena these conditions cannot possibly be necessary. It must be necessary, this argument might go, for infralinguistic organisms such as lower animals to represent their world, and, indeed, in order for infralingual humans to come to use language, it must be possible for them to represent the conventions of their linguistic community, and this possibility cannot presuppose the very language they are learning, on pain of regress. Thus, one might conclude, there must be some form of representation suitable as an account of the character of internal psychological phenomena that does not require the conventional, or perhaps even the causal, embedding that linguistic represenatation requires. (See Fodor 1979 and Churchland 1979 for very different versions of this argument.) An account of the ontology of such phenomena might well be individualistic. As this argument, were it to be successful, would undermine much of the discussion thus far, I will pause to disarm it.

I said above that for now I want to concentrate on the representational states and processes of language-using adult humans, and to defer questions about phylogenetically and ontogenetically more primitive psychological subjects. Indeed a detailed discussion of these matters will be undertaken in chapter 6 and 7, after more of the groundwork has been laid. For now, two things deserve note: First, the states that are members of the sophisticated networks of psychological states and processes into which language users are capable of entering may well turn out to be the only states that are PAs in the full sense and that can be taken to be representational in the fullest sense of that term. We may well need to distinguish more primitive grades of representational character and more primitive psychological phenomena than PAs in order to characterize more primitive cognitive systems. Second, however, even these more primitive phenomena will necessarily partake of the relational character that, we have seen, undergirds any phenomenon when characterized *qua* representation, simply because, waiving the question of the specific character of the reference-making relation, any representational state must be a relation of its bearer to its content. These arguments were independent of the more epistemological arguments for the social and normative character of the PAs which adult humans are capable of entertaining. So, even if we were to determine that there were some nonsocial representational phenomena, more primitive than the PAs, which no doubt there must be, this would not suggest that they are susceptible of an analysis by an Individualistic Theory of Meaning, nor would it impugn the more complex social supervenience base of the PAs.

We can now return to our discussion of the moral of Putnam's case. Inasmuch as for a representational object or state (whether psychological or linguistic) to be of a particular type—where type is individuated by content—is for that object or state to bear certain relations to the external phenonmena that are its contents, as well as, in the case of such linguistically articulated states as the PAs, to the linguistic conventions that determine meaning in the society in which the subject of those states is a citizen, the ontological status of PAs cannot be individualistic. A PA supervenes upon a physical (and social) base which transcends the individual organism which is its nominal subject. And this, of course, is just the moral of the discussion in the preceding section.

Casting the argument in this way may make it clearer why, as I said earlier, the argument for the impossibility of reconciliation, in the form of the argument against the possibility of an Individualistic Theory of Meaning, is found already in the considerations that motivate Naturalistic Individualism as opposed to Methodological Solipsism. For we saw Pylyshyn argue that Methodological Solipsism is incapable of explaining intentionally characterized behavior by appeal to internal symbol processing in the absence of an interpretation of the symbols and processes that figure in the explanans. The reason for this inability was that in the absence of such an interpretation,there would be no explanation of why *those* symbols and processes were related to *that* behavior. (This can be seen as an accusation against the Methodological Solipsist of committing a semantic version of the naturalistic fallacy—of explaining the intentional by reference to the physical.) And, Pylyshyn argues, there is no way of arriving at a justifiable, realistically interpretable assignment of content to a subject's psychological states and processes without taking account of naturalistic data, because the content of these phenomena depends critically upon the relations they bear to their subjects' environment, perception, and behavior.

What I have done (and what is implicit in the accounts of the later Wittgenstein, of Sellars, and of Putnam) is to derive from this insight about the epistemology of PA attributions an ontological moral. If PAs are to be classified by their content, and if their content is *determined* (as opposed to merely made evident) by the relations these states bear to facts beyond the boundary of the organism, as the examples and arguments I have adduced indicate they are, then the correct way to describe these phenomena ontologically would be as relations between their bearers and their environments, and hence as incapable of being characterized by an Individualistic Theory of Meaning. Hence, I would argue, the real conclusion to be drawn from Pylyshyn's defense of Naturalistic Individualism is not that one must be a naturalist about one's epistemology and an individualist about one's ontology, but rather that, if one is to use the language of the PAs, one is committed to a thoroughly naturalistic (that is, nonindividualistic) ontology of mind.

Where does this leave us? In this chapter I have considered and ultimately rejected the possibility of reconciling a realistic position with regard to the existence of the PAs (conceived of as psychological states individuated by reference to contents as specified by something like *that*-clauses) with an individualist, functionalist ontology of psychological phenomena. Such a reconciliation is envisioned both by Methodological Solipsism and by Naturalistic Individualism, but both, we have seen, are committed to an untenable thesis about the ontology of representational phenomena, viz., that they can be construed individualistically.

The impossibility of such a reconciliation, which was, in a different way and for different reasons, envisioned by both Stich (1983) and Churchland (1979, 1981), leaves us with a dilemma: We can cleave to the individualist ontology of mind embodied by functionalism, contemporary work in cognitive science, and neuroscience-based psychology and jettison the PAs from the ontology of the science, arguing that their status is ultimately (like that of phlogiston or perhaps that of Santa Claus) the status of theoretical entities posited by a false theory or, worse, the status of mythical denizens of a false, atheoretical world view; or we can cleave to an ontology of mind including such content-individuated phenomena as the PAs but reject the individualist ontology and methodology embodied by computational theories of mind and approaches to psychology.

The first horn of the dilemma is, of course, that grasped by what I have characterized as eliminativism, comprising both Eliminative Computationalism and Eliminative Materialism. These views agree in their rejection of the PAs as objects suitable as explananda for psychology, or as, in any recognizable form, phenomena suitable to posit in respectable scientific explanations. But while they agree in this rejection, they differ on the fate of the computational paradigm. Eliminative Computationalism, as its name suggests, is a version of computationalism, of cognitivism in psychology, though one radical in its rejection of the Representational Theory of Mind. Eliminative Materialism, on the other hand, rejects the computational paradigm wholesale in favor of a thoroughly neuroscientific psychology. The psychology thus envisioned would contain, and would explain, no phenomena characterized by reference to sentential contents.

To grasp the other horn of the dilemma is to adopt a view perhaps even more discordant with the dominant ideology of cognitive science (though perhaps more in accord with its practice than is the dominant ideology). It is to adopt a vision of the domain of even cognitive psychology as comprising relations of sentient organisms to one another and to their environments, and to forgo the hope of explaining representational phenomena simply in terms of their instantiation in biologically realized information-processing systems. In chapter 6 I will argue that the elimination of the PAs from the ontology and the explanatory domain of psychology is as impossible as their reconciliation with such a domain construed individualistically. In doing so, I will to some extent gloss over the very real differences between Eliminative Computationalism and Eliminative Materialism. In particular, I will be concerned simply to argue for the necessity of something like the PAs—of phenomena characterized by reference to content—in any psychological theory of cognition, and to demonstrate that, whatever the phenomena with which an eliminativist approach proposes to replace the PAs, those entities will be insufficient for their explanatory task. This will set the stage for a sketch of a relational treatment of the PAs and of the nature of a psychology that takes such a treatment seriously.

Chapter 6
The Impossibility of Elimination

It is now time to bring chapter 2's discussion of the relation between the scientific and manifest images to bear on the issue before us. Recall the distinction between the two images as I have characterized them: The manifest image is that in which persons, their actions and institutions *qua* actions and institutions, and the middle-sized perceptibles of our everyday world are to be found. It is a world that spontaneously presents itself to us in perception and conception mediated only by our shared common sense. The scientific image, by contrast, is the image in which the theoretical constructs employed by science in order to explain the regularities observed in the manifest image are to be found. The manifest image contains the conceptual resources to pose problems which it lacks the resources to answer. Thus, electrons, quarks, nutrient gradients, and short-term memory registers are posited, and, as theories gain confirmation, an ontology of the world as conceived of by science emerges.

Against the backdrop of this distinction, and of the competition between the images for the position of ontological arbiter, we can see the position characterized as "scientism" in chapter 2 as underlying the eliminativism of such theorists as Churchland and Stich. Both Eliminative Computationalism and Eliminative Materialism, despite the differences that divide them, are committed to the view that there is no such thing as a propositional attitude, in virtue of the impossibility of the accommodation of the PAs within the ontology of science. Each arrives at this conclusion through arguments involving assertions about the role and nature of science as arbiter of ontology and about the prospects for the PAs in the envisioned structure of science.

We have seen that, according to either version of eliminativism, for there *really to be* PAs would be for them to appear in the theoretical ontology of a scientific psychology. Their appearance, on these views, in the world of commonsense is utterly beside the point when considerations of their ultimate reality are at issue, for on both views our commonsense view of our psychology has the status of a theory—indeed, of a radically inadequate, shallow, and provably false theory. And such a wildly false theory can have no claims on our credence in the reality of its theoretical posits.

Science is, on this view, the sole arbiter of what is that it is and of what is not that it is not.

To be sure, while Eliminative Computationalism envisions the relevant science to be one cast in computational terms, Eliminative Materialism envisions that it will be neurobiological in nature. But each (correctly, I have argued) embodies the view that no psychology meeting its individualistic metascientific strictures can accommodate anything like the PAs as they make their appearance in commonsense, or "folk" psychology. It is in this reliance upon the nonappearance of the PAs within this unified scientific image as a premise from which their nonexistence is argued that eliminativism embodies scientism. Let us now quickly review the principal eliminativist arguments for the nonappearance of the PAs within properly scientific psychology, so that the scientist picture that will be our target will be fully in view.

There are four main arguments. The first, wielded principally by Stich, had to do with the essential vagueness and observer-relativity of PA ascriptions. It was argued that, inasmuch as what is apparently PA identity can be no more than similarity on an indefinite number of dimensions, there can be no criterion of applicability of any PA predicate sufficiently precise for a science. Further, it was argued, inasmuch as the truth conditions (such as they are on this account) for any PA ascription involve the similarity of the attributed PA to a psychological state of the ascriber which he or she *would* express using the same embedded content clause, the applicability of these predicates is observer-relative in a way that is incompatible with the conduct of an objective science.

Second, it was argued, the folk theory is shallow, narrow, and false within its domain. It is incapable of deepening its explanations to provide ever more powerful generalizations, or to link them with underlying biological generalizations. Whole ranges of psychological phenomena, such as those connected with sleep and with psychopathology, are left unexplained. And its generalizations are plagued by disconfirming instances which are all too easy to construct. Tom may desire food and believe that what is in front of him is food, but fail to eat it, say because of a competing desire. And, the argument goes, any attempt to remedy these failures results in the theory's lapsing into vacuity.

Third, the theory is charged, especially by Churchland, with being a theoretical wallflower at the great party of the unity of science. According to this complaint, the physical and biological sciences are converging on a single, unified model of the structure of the physical universe and a synthesis of their respective generalizations and vocabularies. However, on this view, the intentional vocabulary and ontology of psychology (including, according to Churchland, computational psychology) resist inclusion in this growing synthesis. Hence, given the account of the primacy of science in ontology, which underlies this argument, there is strong reason to be suspicious of the reality of the posits of this orthogonal science.

Finally, we considered the argument from the alleged "infralingual catastrophe" It has been argued by eliminativists that a psychology that takes the PAs seriously will fail in two ways to account for the psychological states and processes of infralinguals: First, there is the problem that the contents of PAs—*that*-clauses—are linguistic in character, and it is difficult to come up with an account of the psychological states of infralinguals that relates them directly to such linguistic objects. Second, since we humans are ontogenetically and phylogenetically continuous with many infralingual creatures, we would expect our psychology to be continuous with theirs. But if ours crucially involves states and processes that are linguistic in character, and theirs does not, this would violate the presumed continuity.

All four of these arguments must be seen as arguments against the possibility of locating the PAs within the scientific image. What gives them their bite against the reality of the PAs, however, is the further premise that it is in virtue of occurring in the context of a scientific theory that an expression is capable of referring to an entity or a class of entities, and that it is the truth of that theory that makes it possible for the entity or entities so designated to count as real (or, in a richer version to be discussed below, that it is in virtue of being token-identical with an entity referred to by an expression in an appropriate theory). Much of the remainder of this chapter will be devoted to calling this premise into question and to developing an alternative account of the ontology of the manifest image and of the place of the PAs and the science of psychology with respect to that ontology.

Two of these arguments, however, were they to be successful, would cut more deeply against the reality of the PAs than that—viz., the first (the argument from vagueness and observer-relativity) and the fourth (the argument from the infralingual catastrophe). After saying a few words about this difference in import; I shall defer consideration of these two arguments until chapter 7, where I will develop an alternative sketch of the PAs and their psychology that will meet these objections. The argument from vagueness and subjectivity would be problematic even for an account of the PAs according to which their ontological anchor is cast outside of the purview of science, because it suggests that there is a "mushiness" in the PA concepts that might well reflect nothing so much as a coverup of a lack of understanding of the "real" psychological phenomena underlying human behavior. The argument from infralingual catastrophe is critical because, whatever we say about the nature of the PAs and about the nature of psychology, we must be clear about the relation between the psychology of language users and the psychology of infralinguals, and though there may be (as I will argue) some interesting discontinuities between them, the continuities must be accounted for as well. It is hence a demand on any account of the PAs and their psychology that it give a relatively clear account of their nature, and that it provide an account of a psychology that can do justice to the place of humans and other language users in a broader psychological universe of discourse.

In the remainder of this chapter, I will argue directly against the possibility of eliminating the PAs from our ontology and from the domain of psychology. I will first argue for the irreplaceability of the manifest image as a whole by the scientific image, claiming that the reality of the manifest image is presupposed by the intelligibility of the scientific enterprise. I will then discuss the reasons that the PAs are required in the ontology of that image, and the reasons that it would be mistaken to locate them, at least *ab initio*, in the scientific image. Finally, I will consider the vexed problem of the demands that the PAs make on the enterprise of psychology. Here I will be concerned with their role both as explananda for such a science and as models of the theoretical entities that figure in its explanations. This will set the stage for the discussion of the form that a theory of the PAs might take, and of the nature of a psychology that takes them seriously.

The argument for the necessity of according the manifest image coequal ontological status with the scientific image (a significant departure from Sellars's view) will take the form of a transcendental argument (or, perhaps more accurately, several transcendental arguments) in Kant's sense. That is, I will argue that it is a necessary condition of the intelligibility of the scientific image of the world, and of the scientific enterprise that develops and vindicates it, that the ontology of the manifest image be regarded as real. Any rejection of the reality of the furniture of the manifest image would undermine and render unintelligible the claims of science. I will offer three arguments of this form: one that focuses on the intelligibility of scientific language and activity; one that focuses on the nature of the data that ultimately confirm or disconfirm, thus giving empirical content to, scientific theories; and one concerning the provenance of the concepts and predicates employed by scientific theories.

The enterprise of science—of constructing the scientific image of the world and of the place of humans in it—involves, *inter alia*, the assertion of general statements (the elements of theories), the framing of hypotheses, the testing of hypotheses against evidence, and the occasional confirmation or disconfirmation of hypotheses by experiments. All this epistemic activity gets its point (on the realistic construal of science I am adopting in this study) from its presumed efficacy at getting more and more of the truth about the nature of the world and from its utility in explaining those phenomena we cannot explain without the theoretical apparatus (both conceptual and physical) of science. But, of course, explanations are genuine only to the degree that their explanans are at least approximately true.

And explanations are given only to the extent that the statements comprised by their explanans are asserted. And they issue in understanding only to the extent that they are believed.

If this account of the location of the enterprise of science in the universe of human activity is anywhere near correct, then, regardless of what the details of a philosophical account of that enterprise would have to look like, any account of the intelligibility of science must either (1) take for granted the fact that theories are capable of being believed, of being sincerely asserted, and of being in error (erroneously believed), and that they can issue in understanding (which presumably involves their production of a complex set of PAs in the members of the scientific community and ultimately the lay community or (2) provide an alternative account of the point and the nature of the enterprise, not presupposing the reality of the PAs. If (1) is adopted, then, regardless of whether the PAs appear in the theoretical ontology of any science, their reality in some sense independent of the truth or content of any particular scientific theory is granted as a precondition of the scientific enterprise. Thus, if elimination is possible, (2) must be the route chosen.

But what would such an account look like? We would need an explanation of how theories could be meaningful in the absence of any belief that tokens expressing them have content; an explanation of the explanatory power of theories in the absence of their power to produce beliefs in those considering them; an explanation of the epistemological point of science in a world wherein there is no belief, let alone a practice for its justification, testing, and criticism; and an explanation of scientific error and success that did not analyze these in terms of truly or falsely believing a theory.

It may be instructive (though perhaps an unfair *ad hominem*, if such an argument is indeed possible) to examine the prospects along these lines offered by such eliminativists as Stich and Churchland. Stich frankly admits that

> Deprived of its empirical underpinnings [in folk psychology], our age-old conception of the universe within will crumble just as certainly as the venerable conception of the external universe crumbled during the Renaissance. But that analogy ultimately suggests an optimistic conclusion. The picture of the external universe that has emerged from the rubble of the geocentric view is more beautiful, more powerful, and more satisfying than anything Aristotle or Dante could imagine. Moreover, the path from Copernicus to the present has been full of high intellectual adventure. The thrust of my argument is that we may be poised to begin a similar adventure. (1983, p. 246)

Though none could doubt the invigorating nature of standing on such an intellectual frontier, it is nonetheless prudent to ask for a hint concerning the intelligibility of the quest upon which one is about to embark, and here Stich is silent. Presumably the theories that will deliver the replacement ontology of mind will do so in virtue of being accepted. But what is acceptance if not belief? Presumably they will provide us with a deeper understanding of the nature of mind. But what is the relevant analysis of understanding? It is quite plausible—and this is surely the very large kernel of truth in Stich's vision—that the ontology of psychology, as it deepens its analysis, will include all sorts of theoretical entities as yet undreamed of. This has been true of the development of every natural and social science. But it does not follow from this—nor would it follow even from the complete absence of the PAs from such an ontology—that their eliminability in the manifest image, or the eliminability of that image as a whole, would be a possibility. And if it is the explanation of manifest phenomena that is the goal of a science, the PAs might still make considerable demands on the conduct of psychology.

Churchland is a bit more specific concerning the possible post-PA future of our image of the psychological world. After arguing for a neural ontology of mind, he asks "How will such people understand and conceive of other individuals?" (Here, I suppose, Churchland is *speaking* with the vulgar.) "To this question," he continues, "I can only answer, 'In roughly the same fashion that your right hemisphere 'understands' and 'conceives of' your left hemisphere—intimately and efficiently, but not propositionally!'" (1981, p. 88) However, as Baker (forthcoming) points out, it is far from clear that cerebral hemispheres "understand" or "conceive of" anything, and Churchland's use of the scare quotes indeed implicitly concedes this point. What is more, there is no glimmer of an analysis offered of what nonpropositional understanding or conception could be. In his 1979 book, Churchland suggests that an appropriate model for epistemic categories is to be found in the adaptation of a marine mollusk to a tidal environment, but much work is to be done in order to demonstrate that this adaptation is of an epistemological piece with theoretical scientific knowledge.

It is surely not a demonstrative argument against the possibility of a nonpropositional epistemological foundation of science that no eliminativist has proposed a serious, well-worked-out candidate. Formally, this is nothing more than an *ignoratio*. But I make two apologies for it: First, there is a suggestion that there is a pattern of failure here—that any theory, in order to be explanatory, as opposed to merely deductively successful, must be capable of affecting our PAs. Second, there is a matter of where the burden of proof lies. There is a lengthy epistemological tradition, continued in contemporary philosophy of science, that knowledge involves belief, and that science is, above all, justified in that it provides us with the best possible justifications for belief, and hence the best hope for knowledge.

Anyone proposing so radical a departure from such a model of the human epistemic enterprise must assume the burden of at least charting the alternative course.

The second of the three transcendental arguments I offer concerns the nature of the evidential base of scientific theories. In order for a scientific theory to have empirical content, it must be possible to test its predictions against observations. (This is, of course, too simple, but it will do for present purposes.) Now, the observations relevant to the testing of sophisticated theories are quite often themselves enmeshed with sophisticated theoretical accounts of the nature of instrumentation, and there is no distinction that can be drawn between theoretical and observation language (a point that has now become a commonplace). But this should not obscure the quite independent point that human perception is essential to the process of observation, however theory-laden, and hence to the confirmation or disconfirmation of any scientific theory. And, of course, part and parcel of the attack on the distinction between theory and observation is the insight that perception, as opposed to mere sensory affection, is conceptually enriched sensory awareness, and issues in perceptual belief. And, since what is at issue in experimental observation is the truth or falsity of scientific claims, it is critical that perception issue in something whose truth value can be compared against that of the theoretical prediction that is the consequence of the theory at the bar, and what better than the embedded sentence of a perceptual belief issuing from the relevant observation?

What this means is that it is a demand on scientific theories, as instruments of knowledge, that they contact, via their predictions, the predicates and perceptibles of the manifest image. Hence, it is necessary to take seriously the claims of the ontology of that image to reality, and to take seriously the claims to truth of assertions about its furniture, in order to make sense of the empirical content of scientific theories. But if this line of reasoning is right, it means more than that—it means that, in order to assign empirical content to scientific theories, one must assume the reality of perception and belief. For without them it is hard to see what an account of theory testing would look like.

Before considering the reasons for locating the PAs in the manifest image, and hence for freeing them ontologically from the constraints of psychological theory, I want to offer a last argument for the necessity of taking the manifest image seriously in order to make sense of the scientific image. Here I want to consider the origin of the concepts that make science possible. This argument will be the sketchiest of the three, for any complete development would take us far afield in the philosophy of science. The theoretical predicates of well-developed natural sciences express concepts many of which are far removed from those of common-sense in precision, abstractness, and connectedness to other concepts. For example, the concept of an elementary particle (for example, a neutrino) is far more precise and abstract, and far more embedded in a theory and less connected to a host of everyday concepts, than that of a particle of sand. Nonetheless, the ability of these rarified scientific concepts to explain—to induce understanding—derives from their origin in, and their gradual refinement from, the mundane concepts of the manifest image. Hence, the concept of an elementary particle is a refinement of the concept of a material object, the concept of a force is a refinement of that of a push, and so on. Were there to be no cognitive significance, no content, or no reference for the predicates of the manifest image out of which scientific predicates grow, there would be no possibility of science's fulfilling its function of engendering understanding, and hence no intelligibility to the enterprise.

This argument is somewhat tendentious, but I sketch it here because it suggests a way of understanding the information processes that are the posits of computational psychology as attenuations of the PAs of the manifest image. I will develop this idea more in the next chapter, but this argument and the view about the origin of scientifc concepts it presupposes should serve in part to introduce it.

I want to argue that the ontological allegiance the PAs owe is to the manifest image and to their place therein, rather than to the scientific image. The reason for this is that I wish to disarm the argument that suggests that, because the PAs will not figure in the ontology of an articulated science of psychology, and because psychology is, *qua* scientific, the bailiff of the mental, the arbiter of the reality of mental phenomena, the PAs do not exist. If I am successful in showing that the manifest image has a prior, ineliminable ontological claim to the reality of its essential furniture, and that the PAs are among that essential furniture, I will have shown that, whatever the PAs' status in a finished psychology, their reality cannot be so easily impugned.

There are two sorts of arguments that have been offered to the effect that the PAs belong to the scientific image, and hence that their fate is tied to that of the theories that posit them. The first, due to Sellars (1956), arises from the celebrated "myth of Jones"; the second is offered in various forms by Stich (1983) and Churchland (1979, 1981). Disarming these arguments will elucidate the considerations that lead me to locate the PAs in the manifest image.

According to the myth of Jones, psychological states such as PAs are *posited*, and are construed as "internal" utterances, or, on a more sophisticated view, as short-term-propensities-to-utter. They are posited in order to explain intelligent behavior that *would be comprehensible if it were guided by overt utterance*. Hence, on this view, the semantic and descriptive categories appropriate to overt speech, characterized in the Sellarsian fashion I introduced in the preceding chapter and in chapter 2, characterize objects in the manifest image which are available to us pretheoretically. These include episodes of overt, meaningful speech, particularly in its role as a guide to behavior and a response to perception. But the internal episodes we posit make their entrance as part of a *theory* proposed in order to explain behavior in the absence of these typical meaningful accompaniments. As unobservable posits, these entities deserve our credence only to the extent that the theories that posit them deserve our assent.

Stich and Churchland, inspired by this Sellarsian account, offer similar sets of considerations in favor of construing the PAs and other such psychological phenomena as theoretical posits. As we have already encountered these arguments in a slightly different context in Chapter 4, I will be brief in setting them out here. They argue that the language of everyday psychological description has as both *raison d'être* and semantic bedrock an implicit, widely held (albeit ultimately false) theory of the causation of human behavior: folk psychology, as Stich calls it, or the person-theory, as Churchland calls it. On this account, the meanings of all of the terms in these theories are dependent, as are those of theoretical terms generally, on the content of the theoretical claims in which those terms figure. Churchland gets at it this way:

> Consider ... the set of generalizations whose justification is at issue— the set of sentences descriptive of the general relations holding between (a) types of causal circumstances and types of psychological states (hereafter: P-states), (b) the various types of P-states themselves, and (c) types of P-states and types of overt behavior. We need only think of this set of general statements as a *theory* of the inner dynamics of human beings, as a detailed *hypothesis* concerning the determinants of human behavior, as a theory whose credibility is a direct function of how well it allows us to explain and predict the continuing behavior of individual human beings. If its prowess in these respects proves considerable, then one has paradigmatically good reason for accepting that dynamical theory as true: for supposing that humans are indeed subject to the kinds of states posited by the theory, and that our behavior is a function thereof as the theory describes. And one would have these reasons, note, *independently* of any appeal to the facts of one's own case. Conceivably, the facts of one's own case might even be very *different* from what the theory asserts.... (1979, p. 91)

On this account, any credence we place in the existence of such commonsense psychological phenomena as the PAs can be justified only by appeal to an explanatorily successful theory positing them as theoretical entities necessary for the explanation of behavior. Any attempt to accord them some kind of extratheoretical ontological status, asserts Churchland, would raise serious epistemological problems regarding our knowledge of others' minds, and would render our account of introspection so radically discontinuous with any account of perception that it would be seriously threatened with incoherence. The only alternative to this theoretical account of the nature of the PAs, Churchland argues, is one according to which they are directly introspected. However, such direct introspection stands in marked contrast to any plausible account of perception, and is impossible in the case of the psychological states and processes of others.

Stich's reasons for locating the PAs (if anywhere) in the ontology of science are a bit more indirect, He notes that the nonappearance of a particular predicate in the vocabulary of science is insufficient to warrant the conclusion that its extension is null (his examples include "is a bed slept in by George Washington"). But, he argues, what explains the existence of the objects comprised by the classes denoted by the these predicates, while not the existence of natural kinds corresponding to those classes, is the existence in the ontology of science of a token object identical with each object contained in the class. So. e.g., there is some object describable in the vocabulary of physical science identical with each of the beds in which Washington slept, though there may be no natural kind coextensive with the class of such beds. Given such an ontologically respectable supervenience base, Stich concludes, we can safely assert that such beds exist.

With the PAs, however, the case is somewhat different. The burden of Stich's argument, as we saw in chapter 4, was that there is, in general, no fact of the matter as to what is denoted by a PA attribution—that these attributions fail to pick out identifiable states. Hence, Stich argues, the salvation of the reality of their putative referents by the truth of some token-identity theory concerning the relation they bear to phenomena identified in the vocabulary of science is impossible. (See Stich 1983, chapters 10 and 11.) These are potent arguments in support of the primary location of the PAs as understood by commonsense "folk psychology" in the ontology of science, and hence, given the impossibility of reconciliation, for their nonexistence. If we are to argue for their reality, and for their constraint of psychology and the ontology of mind, we must hence argue head-on against this ontological location. I will reply first to the Sellarsian argument, and then to its cousins in the hands of Stich and Churchland.

There are two reasons for thinking that the account of inner conceptual episodes as theoretical entities modeled on overt speech, as articulated in the myth of Jones, should not convince us of their status as objects of the scientific image. The first has to do with the degree to which they become manifest in introspection once the move to a language of the inner is made.

The second has to do with the fundamental role these phenomena come to play in any conceptual scheme that posits them.

The manifest image is not static. If we thought that our perceptual processes were perfectly rigid, perhaps because of a conflation of perception with sensation, we might think that what we are capable of perceiving is forever fixed by biology. But the realization that perception is a complex interaction of conception and sensation, coupled with the recognition of the plasticity of conception, forces us to conceive of perception as plastic. Given this plasticity, things that may require theoretical activity in order to make their way into everyday perceptual consciousness may come to be manifest themselves as noninferentially perceptibles at a later stage of collective or individual conceptual development. (See Churchland 1979, chapter 2.) Hence, the fact that pre-Jonesians did not posit PAs, and that for Jones and his contemporaries they did have the status of theoretical entities, does not entail that this status must attach to them for all time. In fact, at later stages of the myth of Jones we learn that the post-Jonesians become so adept with Jonesian language that they begin spontaneously to ascribe PAs to themselves, without any theoretical activity. Their introspective consciousness has, I suggest, undergone a dramatic transformation.

Once post-Jonesian culture and post-Jonesian persons have absorbed the language of the PAs to the extent that they spontaneously and noninferentially respond to their own inner events and states in terms of the categories of that language, the correct description of their image of themselves, and of their inner psychological processes *as they manifest themselves to themselves*, is in terms of these psychological categories. The migration of their consciousness is equally characterizable as the transformation of a set of predicates from the scientific to the manifest language and, in the material mode, as the transformation of a set of phenomena from the status of theoretical entities to that of readily perceptible entities.

It might be suggested at this point that the distinction I am relying on between the manifest and scientific images, the location of PAs on the manifest side, and my characterization of them as "noninferentially perceived" constitute a flirtation with, or even a seduction by, a form of the "myth of the given." A casual reading might give the impression that I am characterizing representational phenomena *as presenting themselves to introspection as representational*, or, worse, *as representing their contents* (where "their contents" is taken *de re*). But this is not what I have in mind. The introspective awareness of our own representational states *as representational*, like our awareness of such states in others, is, to be sure, a conceptual response to whatever affects our proprioceptive sense. What makes this perception, like the perception of tables and chairs (which likewise do not present *themselves* to us *as tables and chairs*) noninferential is the spontaneity and the automatic nature of the conceptual activity involved in the perceptual cycle, a feature of that activity which distinguishes it from the highly theoretical activity involved in, say, "perceiving" an elementary particle in an accelerator. (To be sure, the precise location of the divide between the images is, on this account, a pragmatic matter. That is as it should be. But the *existence* of such a divide, and the location of the PAs on the manifest side, at least *ab initio*, is a conceptual matter, as I have argued above.)

But this transformation might be seen—as it is by eliminativists of a Sellarsian persuasion—as one of a series of such transformations of the respective ontologies of the manifest and scientific images, the next of which will import to the manifest image a radically different set of psychological phenomena and will simultaneously jettison the outworn language of the PAs with which it is currently burdened. But there is something special about the Jonesian revolution which issues in the necessity of any manifest image's retaining the phenomena it first recognized: It is in that revolution that persons first emerged as epistemic subjects and actors capable of entertaining scientific discourse at all. So we can say that the manifest image that presents itself in opposition to the scientific image—that makes the demands that require that image, and that provides the methodological canon for it—comes to be, and so with it the grounds of the possibility of science, with the entrance of the PAs into the manifest image. The world as it manifests itself to us, pretheoretically, is a world in which we are the subjects of psychological states which include (among others) the PAs, and for this reason, whatever the theoretical underpinnings of the introspective consciousness that so spontaneously delivers our contentful inner states to us, these contentful states must be accorded their primary status as objects of the manifest image. And this, of course, is a matter of ontology, not merely of epistemology.

With this preliminary skirmish, which removes some of the eliminativist sting from the Sellarsian account of the theoretical underpinnings of the ontology of introspective consciousness, we can consider some of the reasons why the eliminativist arguments locating the PAs in the ontology of science are mistaken. The first reason is that if the alleged theory of which they are a part—the P-theory, or folk psychology—were to be seriously presented as a *theory* of human behavior, as part of an ongoing scientific research program, would be so ludicrously and obviously false that it would have been rejected eons ago. (See Baker [forthcoming].) Churchland and Stich both harp on its falsity, and deride their opponents for failing to note it, but they miss the significance of the obviousness of that falsity.

Given any catalog of "laws" of folk psychology, such as the ones offered by Churchland (1979, 1981) and Stich (1983), it is painfully easy to generate falsifying instances of any of them. That such laws are empirically false, if taken to range over actual individuals, is not a new insight. It lies behind any nonexternalist account of epistemology. But the moral of this falsity, for our present purposes, is this: If those who have used intentional language, including the language of the PAs, in characterizing themselves and their fellows, over at least the last four millenia, have thought that the truth of their attributions depended upon the truth of something like the P-theory, where "theoretical truth" in this context involves at least empirical well-confirmedness, then they have been either wildly insincere or remarkably stupid. It makes more sense to assume that this language was not being used as theoretical language whose semantics depends upon a theory in which its terms are embedded, but rather as language in the manifest image, whose semantics depends on much broader community conventions. (This is certainly part of the moral of the philosophy of the later Wittgenstein.)

This leads us directly to a second reason for rejecting eliminativist arguments in favor of locating the PAs within the theoretical ontology of a false theory. The account of the semantics of theoretical terms presupposed by this arguments is, roughly speaking, that of Putnam (1975a). On such a theory, there is a "division of linguistic labor" in the assignment of meaning to such terms, whereby a "community of experts," such as the scientific community in a particular field, determines the intension of a theoretical term. So, presumably, chemists here on Earth are charged with determining that "water" refers to H_2O, whereas zoologists determine what counts as a tiger. So, presumably, if the terms of folk psychology that ostensibly refer to psychological phenomena get their meaning in a similar way, there must be a relevant community of experts who determine what counts as a belief, a hope, a fear, a desire, a pain, and all of these supposedly theoretical terms. But there has never been a community of experts in folk psychology (unless twentieth-century analytic philosophers count). Cognitive psychologists have never pretended to be up to this semantic task, nor have their predecessors in behaviorism or structuralism. The terms denoting inner entities of psychology, when they have been plausibly assigned meaning on a Putnam model, have been far more explicitly theoretical, including such terms as "Drive", "visual buffer", and "cathexis". On examination, it would seem that the semantic history of the terms of "folk psychology" is far more like that of the other terms of the manifest image than like those of scientific terms.

A closely related point distinguishing the semantic behavior of folk-psychological terms from that of *prima facie* theoretical terms is the insensitivity of the language of folk psychology to experimental results. For instance, a theoretical term like "neutron" may change its meaning in physics as our conception of the microstructure of the atom evolves. At one time, the most accurate explication of its meaning might have been something like "primitive elementary particle of atomic weight 1.0, with a neutral charge", whereas now the story is much more complicated, and "neutron" denotes a class of composite objects. Similarly, the explicitly theoretical terms of psychology have always this sensitivity to experimental evidence. (Consider for instance the evolution of the meaning of the term "Drive", in the hands of Hull, Spence, and Tolman, from a term denoting a presumed physiological quantity to a highly abstract characterization of a functional state of an organism. (See Hull 1943; Tolman 1932, 1943.) But what experimental results would convince us to change the meanings of the terms of folk psychology? Even those who assert their theoretical character note their persistence with much the same meaning despite the constant flux of psychological theory over the past century. This insensitivity is shared by most terms whose meanings are fixed in the manifest image. It should serve as more evidence that the location of these expressions in the language of science is mistaken. This is not, of course, to say that there is no evolution in the meanings of the terms employed by folk psychology, or that there is no evolution in the sophisticated philosophy of mind concerned with them. The manifest image, as I noted earlier, is far from static, and indeed evolves frequently under scientific pressure. Rather, the point is that the forces governing the evolution of the meanings of these terms are different in kind from those governing the semantic evolution of scientific terms, and that however they evolve, our self-conception as epistemic subjects requires ascribing to ourselves representational states with propositional contents, and inferential processes operating thereon.

All of this tempts me to an *ad hominem*: A central feature of eliminativist complaints against the PAs is that the language ascribing them is vague, subject to one's point of view, and orthogonal to the more regimented language of the scientific image. It is odd, then, that anyone advancing this complaint—in effect, charging the PAs with being the mythical referents of *unscientific* language—would at the same time charge the PAs with nonexistence on the grounds that they are the entities of a false *scientific* *theory*. The eliminativist tries not to have his cake and not to eat it, either. A proper understanding of the quite correct arguments for the nonscientific character of these predicates should reveal not that they are scientific, but that they are not. But then, the central eliminativist premise—that the failure of the PAs to figure in a scientific theory entails their non-existence—is surely false. (See also Gordon 1986 for arguments against locating the PAs in the ontology of science.)

I have argued that the manifest image must be accorded equal ontological status with the scientific image. That is, the reality of the objects, properties, and entities that it posits must not be impugned merely on account of their failure to find a use in scientific theory. I have argued that this ontological status is required in order to render the scientific enterprise, and hence the scientific image of the world, intelligible in the first place. And finally, I have argued that essential to that image, and presupposed by the conduct of science, are the intentional phenomena such as the PAs which figure in our everyday discourse about and introspection of our mental lives, and that eliminativist attempts to anchor these phenomena in the scientific image through a construal of folk psychology as theoretical fail. All of this indicates that the eliminativist enterprise is, in a straightforward sense, self-refuting. It commits, as Baker (forthcoming) has put it, "cognitive suicide" by denying what is necessary in order to give it sense, viz., that those who assert it believe its truth (or, for that matter, anything at all) or mean anything by asserting it.

Before introducing the question of the implications of the view of the ontology of the mental we are developing for psychology, I want to consider Churchland's anticipation of this charge of cognitive suicide. Churchland writes:

> ... the reductio proceeds by pointing out that the statement of eliminative materialism is just a meaningless string of marks or nosies, unless that string is the expression of a certain *belief*, and a certain *intention* to communicate, and a *knowledge* of the grammar of the language, and so forth. But if the statement of eliminative materialism is true, then there are no such states to express. The statement at issue would then be a meaningless string of marks or noises. It would therefore *not* be true. Therefore it is not true. Q.E.D....
>
> The question-begging nature of this move is most graphically illustrated by the following analogue....
>
> The anti-vitalist says that there is no such thing as vital spirit. But this claim is self-refuting. The speaker can expect to be taken seriously only if his claim cannot. For if the claim is true, then the speaker does not have vital spirit, and must be *dead*. But if he is dead, then his statement is a meaningless string of noises, devoid of reason and truth. (1981, pp. 89–90)

But Baker (forthcoming, pp. 24–25) notes that the *reductio* against eliminative materialism and the allegedly parallel failed *reductio* against anti-vitalism are indeed not parallel, and that the respects in which they are not parallel explain the failure of Churchland's lampoon vitalist argument. In the first place, she notes, the vitalist argument takes as an assumption the falsity of anti-vitalism, and argues from that assumption to the nonassertability of the thesis. This is clearly a *petito principii*. But the argument against eliminative materialism assumes, instead, the *truth* of eliminative materialism, and demonstrates on *that* assumption its nonassertability. That is, far from being question-begging, a straightforward *reductio* (assuming of course the necessity of assertability for truth). Hence, the fact that the vitalist lampoon is question-begging in no way impugns the argument against eliminative materialism.

In the second place, Baker argues, there is a dialectically critical difference in the situation of the disputants in the two arguments with respect to the presuppositions they share. The vitalist and the anti-vitalist agree that being alive is a necessary condition of making claims. They are arguing about what it is to be alive. The vitalist argument is absurd because it presupposes an answer to what is at dispute in the guise of merely asserting what is agreed upon. But, Baker notes, the eliminative materialist and his opponent do not agree about the necessity of having beliefs for making assertions. Indeed, this is just what is up for dispute. Far from lumping his opponent with the vitalist in virtue of the anti-eliminativist's assertion that having beliefs is a precondition for making assertions, the eliminativist should class himself with an anti-vitalist who would embrace the claim that the dead can make assertions. The arguments hence fail to be parallel in this respect as well.

I find Baker's rejoinder totally compelling. One further point needs to be made in this regard, however. It might be argued that there is a vicious circularity in my account of the necessity of the reality of the PAs as a condition for the conduct and intelligibility of science. The charge would go as follows: I have argued that the PAs are necessary because in their absence we can tell no coherent story about the possibility of sincere assertion or of error, nor can we make sense of perception in a way that allows it to enter into the testing of theories. But at the same time, I have asserted that the best way to understand the PAs is as intentional tokens whose intentionality is of a piece with, and is to be understood in terms of, the intentionality of linguistic tokens. In this sense, the very linguistic tokens which I suggested presuppose the PAs for their meaningfulness themselves serve as the models for these intentional phenomena. So, the charge goes, I have given the PAs priority in understanding language, including the language of theories, and have at the same time given overt language priority in understanding the PAs.

The circularity, however, is only apparent, for the priority of language over psychological phenomena in this account is an *epistemological* priority— we develop the vocabulary of intentionality and of meaning, and gain our primary understanding of these phenomena, through the consideration of language. The priority of the PAs, however, is an *ontological* priority, for, regardless of the fact that language is our best source of evidence regarding intentional and semantic properties, having a psychology rich enough to have something to express linguistically is surely a necessary condition of language. Actually, the story is a bit more complex than this, but there is sufficient edge to this charge to deserve a preliminary sketch at this point.

The real edge derives not so much from the charge of circularity as from the connection of this worry to the charge of infralinguistic catastrophe, for our account of the primacy of language in an account of intentional inner states is a bit more ontology-laden than the quick reply sketched in the last paragraph revealed. In emphasizing the primacy of rule-governedness and the social basis of rules in the grounding of the meaningfulness of any meaningful phenomena, I have been developing, and postponing the resolution of, a problem about the status of what look awfully like representational phenomena in infralinguals, and about the ontogenesis of representation in humans. Since a psychology rich enough to include representation appears to be a necessary precondition for language, and since public language appears to be a necessary precondition for having PAs, we seem to be beset by a genetic circle that requires more serious consideration than the explanatory circle considered above.

Briefly, the strategy I will adopt in resolving this problem will be to distinguish two grades of intentionality, or representational character. Possessing the more primitive grade will emerge as a feature of psychologically complex systems, even despite their nonparticipation in systems of convention. But systems possessing only this more primitive representational character will not count as believers in the full sense. Linguistic behavior will turn out to be a necessary condition of the higher grade of intentionality, and hence of possessing PAs. Nonetheless, epistemologically, there will be a strong sense in which more richly intentional language will serve as the epistemological *entré* into even the more primitive animal representation.

Now that I have argued that we cannot coherently jettison the ontology of the manifest image, and that it is in this ontological framework that the PAs find their home, it is time to ask just what demands the psychological ontology of the manifest image places on scientific psychology. If the ontology of computational psychology cannot be reconciled with the PAs, just what is the future of such a psychology, and what is the prospect for a more detailed understanding of human cognitive processes that include our PAs? I will argue that, just as the manifest image generally has a role in the formation of scientific problems, in the development of scientific conceptual apparatus, and in the testing of scientific theories, the PAs have such a regulative role in psychology. Moreover, because of the special social nature of the PAs and because of the ontologically naturalistic (that is, nonindividualistic) nature of representational phenomena generally, I will argue that there are special reasons for thinking that psychology must take a more methodologically naturalistic turn than the computational paradigm (or at least that paradigm as construed by its philosophical commentators) has taken to date.

The PAs and other psychological phenomena that inhabit the common-sense framework of psychological description and explanation place the same kind of explanatory demand on scientific psychology that any mani-fest phenomena place on the sciences into whose bailiwicks they fall. Just as chemistry is called upon to explain such occurrences as the solution of sugar in water, astronomy to explain the setting of the sun, and physics to explain the uniform acceleration of falling bodies, and just as a failure to explain these phenomena adequately—despite the fact that they are ini-tially characterized in a language that may be foreign to the science in its eventual articulation—counts as an explanatory failure of the relevant science, so psychology is called upon quite naturally to explain and charac-terize our psychological states as they manifest themselves to us in the world of sophisticated commonsense. A failure to provide some scientific characterization of the phenomena that underlie them would count as an explanatory failure for psychology.

But, as we saw in chapter 5, in order to provide an account of these intentional phenomena, psychology will have to abandon the individualism that underlies both reconciliationist and eliminativist positions. the natural-ism the science would need to adopt would be a thoroughly ontological naturalism according to which the proper objects of at least some psycho-logical study would be the relations the bearers of psychological properties stand in to their environments and the objects of their representational states. This naturalistic demand is a straightforward consequence of the ineliminability of the PAs from the psychological landscape, of the fact that they form the epistemological contact point between cognitive psy-chology and the world of commonsense, and of the fact that they are irreconcilable with an individualistic ontology of the mental.

Finally, as was noted briefly above, there is the problem of the in-fralinguals. There is a *prima facie* continuum of the biological and psycho-logical lives of infralinguals and the linguistically competent. Many of the psychological states and processes of infralinguals are at least apparently intentional, and something like the PA predicates seems called for in char-acterizing those phenomena. But these psychological subjects, while they and their psychological processes are, to be sure, located in natural contexts to which they are related by their psychological states, are not members of communities that adopt conventions and lead them to conform to norms of linguistic and epistemic behavior. I have already sketched, and will develop in more detail in the next chapter, an account of the PAs according to which having them in the full sense depends crucially upon membership in such linguistic communities. Thus, these intentional phenomena will place a twofold demand on psychology, requiring an account of the social foun-dations of human intentional cognitive phenomena and an account of the more primitive but still relational intentional processes of the infralinguals, which presumably underlie our more complex abilities, and the ways in which they undergird linguistic abilities.

However, as we have seen, the manifest image not only places explanatory demands on science; it also provides science with the prototypes of the concepts necessary for theory construction. So just as our manifest image of middle-sized dry goods provides physics with the raw material for the concepts of subatomic particles, we would expect commonsense psychology to provide a science of psychology with the raw material for the construction of its conceptual apparatus. An important part of the account I will develop of the status of both the PAs and the theoretical entities posited by cognitive psychology and artificial intelligence will be the account of the nature and source of the intentionality of subdoxastic but nonetheless representational phenomena.

This sets the program for the positive part of this study. I will develop a general account of the nature of PAs, arguing that PA attributions are in fact to be understood as locating the bearers of PAs in a network of relations to their environment. I will argue that an important part of the task of cognitive science is to explicate the nature of these relationships. The account will also attend to the nature of more primitive intentional states and processes, such as those of infralingual animals and humans and perhaps those of computing machines. I will argue that there is an important sense in which these are the ontologically and ontogenetically primary intentional phenomena, and that they can be treated, as they must be, as independent of any social embedding, despite the fact that they must be construed naturalistically. But, I will suggest, there is still an important sense in which the full-fledged intentional events, states, and processes of language users are epistemically primary in the attribution of even these more primitive phenomena. Finally, I will discuss the relationship that emerges from this account between the study of the individualistically characterizable processes of cognitive systems and the study of their naturalistic properties, and the structure this suggests for psychological research and theory.

Chapter 7

The Place of the Propositional Attitudes in Psychology: A Proposal

I have three principal goals in this chapter, the only chapter in which I make positive claims concerning the ontology and methodology of psychology.

First, I want to offer a sketch of a theory of the nature of the propositional attitudes. The generality issues from the fact that the details of any theory constructed along the lines I present will be matters for empirical cognitive science and not for speculative philosophy of mind. In the course of developing this account, I will return once again to the critical role of language in mental representation and to the critical role of a theory of language in a psychology of representation. I will also return to Fodor's five conditions on such theories, and test mine against them, arguing that it fares rather well.

Second, as I suggested in chapter 6, I will develop the account of intentionality and the place of language in the science of intentional phenomena in more detail. Here I will distinguish two grades of intentionality, one appropriate to the representational states of infralinguals (and perhaps for the subdoxastic information-processing states of language users) and one for the representational states (such as the PAs) of full-blooded epistemic subjects such as ourselves. This will involve a discussion of the ontogenesis of cognitive capacity, of the relation between the ontology of the PAs and the conditions under which we find it useful to attribute them, and of the difficult matter of the senses in which the capacity for PAs is presupposed by the capacity for language and in which the capacity for language is presupposed by the capacity for PAs.

Third, I will discuss the future shape of cognitive psychology, and of cognitive science more generally, in light of the argument developed in the first two sections of this chapter and in the two preceding chapters. The naturalistic, socially, linguistically, and neuroscientifically sensitive future I envision will, I think, seem almost ploddingly familiar to many cognitive psychologists, but it diverges sharply from the solipsistic view of that science taken by most philosophers and many computation-minded psychologists.

We have seen that individualist theories of the PAs cannot succeed. What would a nonindividualist alternative look like? Clearly, on such an account,

PAs will be relations between their bearers and something. But just what a psychological subject is related to, and by what relation he or she is related to it, is by no means as clear. The most likely candidate for the external *relata* of the PAs might seem to be sentences in public languages, given what has been said so far about the origins of the semantic categories by which we characterize psychological states and processes in those we use to characterize public language. Moreover, in Sellars's dot-quote device we have a means for constructing sortals comprising utterances and inscriptions from diverse languages, as well as inner episodes and objects. What is more, as we shall see below and as was hinted above, there is a definite sense in which, in order to have PAs in what I call "the full sense," language is required. But there is an important consideration, connected with the representational states and processes of infralinguals, that suggests that it would be an error to simply identify PAs as relations to linguistic tokens, however functionally characterized.

Construing the PAs simply as relations to public linguistic tokens would introduce, in the interests of epistemological simplicity, an ontological puzzle. While such an account would make it easy to understand the deep parallel (noted in chapter 3) between verbs of saying and verbs of PA-attribution and easy to understand the reason for the necessity of language for PAs in the full sense, it would render the continuity of the psychological processes of language users with those of infralinguals mysterious. For there surely seems to be a sense in which persons who have not acquired language, and animals that will never do so, nonetheless stand in representational relations to their environments that are, in important and relevant senses, of a piece with the PAs, despite the fact that it would be odd to attribute to them any interesting relations to any items of public language. So when a toddler shows every sign of believing that his bottle is in the refrigerator, or when a dog apparently believes that a cat is up the beech tree, our attributions of the relevant PAs presumably do not ascribe to either the toddler or the dog psychologically interesting relations to bits of English (though there may be semantically interesting relations in the background). This suggests that, although linguistic facts may play a central role in the PAs of language users, a simple account according to which they were the sole facts to which their bearers are related by PAs would be too simple.

The supervenience base of PAs (that set of extra-psychological phenomena, whether individualistic or not, upon which they supervene—which are such that any two worlds that would be indistinguishable with respect to them would necessarily be indistinguishable with respect to the PAs it contains) would specify either the necessary and sufficient conditions for, say, having a belief, or even having a belief *that p*, for some *p*, or one that would enumerate the nonintentional phenomena on which such PAs as belief or the belief that p, typically supervene. In fact, I believe, the quest for an account of such a base is quixotic. An explicit, nonintentional, nonsemantic account of the nature or the relata to which we are related by our PAs should not be forthcoming. Consider two examples, one of a full-blooded belief of a language user and one of the more primitive belief of an infralingual: Suppose that I attribute to Jones the belief that most Australian snakes are poisonous. Consider the breadth of the supervenience base of the state I have attributed to him. It will include, no doubt, relations to a number of linguistic types. For instance, he will be disposed to utter, in appropriate circumstances, things like "Most Australian snakes are poisonous," or its equivalent in whatever language he is speaking at the time. His belief, in order to be about Australian snakes, will supervene, as I have argued in chapters 5 and 6, on Australia and its snake population, and, of course, since he expresses it in language, upon the conventions in his language governing the meanings of the words in which he expresses the belief. Alteration of the reference-inducing relations Jones bears to the snakes (with which he may never have come into physical contact), of the meaning-inducing relations Jones bears to his linguistic community (of which he may be blissfully unaware), or of the dispositional relations Jones bears to utterances or to other, nonlinguistic behavior, all of which conspire to vindicate the attribution, would alter the truth value of the belief attribution, even if Jones's individualistically characterized properties remained the same. Fido believes that the cat climbed the tree. He, of course, doesn't express his belief in words. But in attributing this belief to him, we are certainly attributing to him a state that relates him to his environment. It supervenes upon Fido, the cat, the tree, and possibly the chase that is causally responsible for the situation Fido represents. Again, vary the relata and the state varies.

Now, given an account that proposes such a large, irregular, and distinctly non-projectibly-characterizable supervenience base for any representational phenomenon as this, one might reasonably wonder whether anything interesting can be said about the PAs, and whether a science of psychology that takes them seriously is possible. One can interpret Stich's attack on the PAs as embracing something like this account of their ontology and drawing the gloomiest philosophical conclusion, and Davidson 1970a as drawing the gloomy psychological conclusion.) With expectations thus lowered, I will say a few positive things.

In the first place, such ontological awkwardness has not caused consternation in, or hampered the development of, any other social science. Consider economics and cultural anthropology, both arguably close cousins of psychology. Each of these sciences studies a plethora of phenomena essential to its domain which lack "tidy" supervenience bases in exactly the same sense that I am arguing the PAs do. In economics we find such theoretical terms as "deficit", marginal untility", and "balance of payments"; in cultural anthropology, "kinship relation", "family", and "ritual". One only has to consider, in order to see the absurdity involved, the enterprise of giving sets of necessary and sufficient conditions in physical or biological language for any of these, or that of circumscribing the supervenience bases of the process-, event-, or state-types they denote, or those of any tokens of these types.

But anthropology and economics are both thriving sciences, with much to tell us about their domains, and vital theoretical paradigms. Moreover, anthropology, at least, is directly a science of human behavior, and economics, despite the apparent ontological untidiness of its domain, is by now a heavily mathematical science of the artificial ecosystem in which we find ourselves as economic actors. I take it that these examples, while not pvoviding a demonstrative argument suggest that an account of PAs according to which one's PA locates one in a complex, perhaps indefinite network of relations to one's environment and one's cultural and linguistic community would not by itself preclude the development of a science of psychology that would take the PAs seriously. I will also argue by example that much promising research in psychology and other subfields of contemporary cognitive science takes seriously the PAs construed in just this way.

I have said repeatedly, and now I will argue, that one must have mastered a language in order to have psychological states that are representational in a sufficiently rich way to count as PAs in the full sense in which we attribute these states to ourselves and our fellows. There are two reasons for this that can be mobilized at this point: Only via language can one represent abstract entities, and only via language can one be related to the completely imaginary.

I want to argue that sentence 1 entails that John speaks a natural language, in a way that sentence 2 does not entail that Fido does.

(1) John believes that every horse has at least one property possessed by no unicorn.
(2) Fido believes that the cat is up the tree.

John's belief is in part about properties. But properties are abstracta, and hence are things with which John's contact cannot be straightforwardly perceptual. The only device for referring to them, and hence for thinking about them, is language. Hence, only by mastering the abstraction operators in natural language is John able to have inner episodes that function in semantically similar ways. And the same things can be said about the imaginary. Surely we don't want to say that what makes John's belief about unicorns has anything to do with unicorns in its supervenience base.

But it does have a great deal to do with the presence of the word "unicorn" in that supervenience base and with the conventions regarding the use of that word in English. Hence, we see again that, in virtue of facilitating thought about the imaginary, language is a necessary condition of John's belief.

Sentence 2, by contrast, makes no such demands on Fido. His belief, conceptually impoverished as it is, supervenes only on himself, the cat, and the tree (and perhaps on a few other historical facts, but certainly not on any linguistic facts). The external relata of his belief are hence accessible to him directly through perception and action. Hence, sentence 2 attributes to him a relation to the cat and the tree into which he can happily enter in the absence of any vocabulary in which to express it. While his internal state may be a ·The cat is up the tree·, it need not, and indeed cannot, present itself *to him* as such (or at all), though it presents itself to us in that way, given our conceptual apparatus including the concepts of the PAs (and, indeed, I am about to argue, in characterizing it as a ·The cat is up the tree·, if we were to mean this literally we would attribute to Fido too rich a representational structure). And what if there is no cat, and Fido is barking up the wrong tree? Then, while the supervenience base of his current representational state may include no present cat, it will include whatever is causally responsible for the barking.

We can now make a first pass at explaining why the PAs of infralinguals are representational in a somewhat different, more attenuated sense than are ours. The PAs are comprised, along with other representational events, states, and processes, by a system of phenomena that together constitute an organism's map of the world (in the sense of Tolman 1948 and Sellars 1979, 1980, and 1981). But maps, including cognitive maps, come with varying degrees of representational power. Whereas a very sketchy map might reveal only, say, that New York is northeast of Los Angeles, a more detailed version might tell us that they are major cities that stand in certain relations to other urban centers, political boundaries, and geographical features. What gives the most powerful, detailed, and perspicuous cognitive maps their representational power is the fact that their representational elements can interact logically to "fill in" detail not explicitly given in perception or already "stored" in memory. They can be used to hypothesize, and to guide theoretical action. All of this requires that their contents can have the abstractive, inferential, and descriptive power that our linguistically enriched PAs do. To the extent that the elements of a cognitive map fall short of this cognitive power—that is, to the extent that they fall short in point of the expressive and inferential power of natural languages—they will be relatively inadequate to represent the world and to guide rational action in it.

For this reason—that the representational systems of infralinguals are so much less powerful than ours, in the same way that a very sketchy map is so much less powerful than a fully articulated one—it is fair to say that they differ in kind, and that their representational systems, in virtue of lacking the very sorts of structure that give ours the power they have, are of a different order. They are incapable in principle—just as the sketchy map is incapable in principle of representing political facts about New York—of representing much of what we are capable of representing. And it is for this reason that, except in hyperbolic attribution contexts, it is always false to attribute to an infralingual beliefs about the imaginary or the abstract.

Though what I have had to say in positive vein about the nature of the PAs has been extremely general and vague, there is enough on the table that we can test this outline of an account against Fodor's five conditions on a philosophical theory of the PAs. Recall from chapter 3 that these were that any account must treat the PAs as relations between their bearers and something, that the parallelism between the PA verbs and the verbs of saying must be explained, that the opacity of the PAs must be explained, that there must be an explanation of the fact that the contents of the PAs have logical form, and that any theory must harmonize with the results of empirical psychology. Inasmuch as these are reasonable demands on a theory of the PAs, let us consider each of these conditions in turn.

The first condition—that the account must treat the PAs as relational—is satisfied trivially by the approach I advocate, for on this approach to stand in a PA is to be located in a network of relations to such things as the objects (if any) of the PA, one's relevant perceptual and behavioral history, and, in the case of language users, to one's linguistic community and to the linguistic items in which one would express one's PA.

More specifically, and more relevant to Fodor's demand, the PAs are on this view relations of their bearers to linguistic types individuated by their content. This way of specifying these relata avoids the problems raised for other views on which PAs are relations to linguistic tokens. Unlike accounts whereon a believer is related to a token in a particular natural language, this account is not beset with the problems concerning the impossibility of shared beliefs among speakers of different languages. Nor is this view subject to the problems associated with views that require infralinguals to be related to natural-language tokens in order to represent their environments. Finally, unlike Fodor's view, ours is not plagued by an incoherent ontological individualism.

This account also makes it clear just why there is a striking parallel between the PA verbs and the verbs of saying, for to *say* that most Australian snakes are poisonous is to produce a public token of a ·Most Australian snakes are poisonous·, whereas to *believe* that most Australian snakes are poisonous is to produce, or be disposed to produce, an internal token of a ·Most Australian snakes are poisonous·. The ontological accounts I have urged for tokens of public language and of internal psychological states are homogeneous—both involve nonindividualistic supervenience bases. Inasmuch as in the case of full-fledged PAs linguistic items, dispositions, and conventions are central to the bases of both public and "private" assertion, there should be no surprise that these verbs fall into a natural linguistic class.

Discussion of the next two desiderata—those concerning opacity and logical form—requires a detour through the relationship between PA attributions (including self-attributions) and the PAs they attribute. This will be a first pass at this topic, to which we will return a bit later in the context of the promised discussion of Stich's charges of vagueness and objectionable subjectivity against the PA predicates. PAs, as I have argued, are, from the standpoint of ontology states that, while they are discrete individuals within the manifest image, and arguably within the domain of cognitive psychology, supervene on a motley plethora of relations their bearers stand in with respect to their environments. A PA attribution is an assignment of a location in such a network of relations; a PA is such a location.

Now, when we say that PA verbs create opaque contexts, we must ask whether it is the PA itself that is in some sense opaque or whether it is the sentence attributing the PA. When the question is put this way, the answer is plain: Opacity is a property (or perhaps a cluster of properties) of linguistic contexts. In the cases that concern us, it is the PA verb in an attribution-sentence that creates an opaque context. Though this point may seem obvious, its neglect has led Fodor (1978, 1979, 1982) and Lewis (1979) to think that a theory of the *attitudes* is bound to account for this phenomenon, as opposed to a *semantic* theory of *attitude reports*. (Cresswell [1985] succeeds in disentangling this issue, and in providing a compelling treatment of the semantics of attitude reports, while studiously eschewing any conclusions concerning the nature of the states such reports ascribe.)

Attitude reports (typically—we will not consider de re attitude reports, as the issues involved in the various strains of the *de dicto/de re/de expressione/de se* controversies are semantic whereas our questions are ontological) create opaque contexts because, as Kiteley (1968, 1985) has argued, the expressions that fall within the scope of PA verbs function impurely: they occur at the same time referentially and quasi-quotationally, or, as I have put it in this study, as dot-quoted expressions. Consider the following minilogue:

> *John*: Oedipus wanted to marry Jocasta.
> *Bill*: Right. But he didn't want to marry his mom.

Given the identity between Jocasta and Oedipus's mom, we are left with the problem of showing how our theory of the PAs explains the consistency of the PAs attributed by Bill and John.

John ascribes to Oedipus a PA, a psychological state, that—regardless of the nature of its supervenience base (note how completely irrelevant the ontological story about the PAs is to the problem of the opacity of PA attributions)—is characterized by John as an ·I want to marry Jocasta· (that is, as a psychological state that plays the same role in Oedipus's psychology that one which John would report by "I want to marry Jocasta" would play in John's psychology). (Here I am skating over issues concerning the distinction between beliefs and desires. That botanical discussion of the several PAs is beyond the scope of this investigation.) Critical to the specification of this role are the inferential relations into which the states in question enter. Of course, in the absence of a ·Jocasta is my mom· these beliefs would not issue in the occurrence of or the disposition to produce an ·I want to marry my mom·, which is the belief that Bill consistently refrains from attributing to Oedipus.

Now, despite the fact that Oedipus would never characterize his current psychological state as one of wanting to marry his mom, and despite the fact that attributing his psychological state to him in this way would fail to predict accurately and to explain much of his behavior (though one has to be careful here—this description will have some predictive power so long as we retain the phrase "Oedipus's mom" as the referring term by which we pick out Jocasta), there is a perfectly good sense in which we can attribute to Oedipus the desire to marry his mom, possibly qualifying the attribution, at least implicitly, with something like "but he doesn't know that it's his mom." However, the possibility of this distinct kind of attribution does not point to a distinct kind of psychological state. Rather, as Cresswell (1985) has argued, it can be explained tidily by reference to the systematic ambiguity of attribution locutions in ordinary language, which can be sensitive to varying degrees of structure in the complement clauses of PA verbs.

Given these considerations, it is fair to say that the account I have been developing of the nature of the PAs and their relation to PA attributions in a way sidesteps, or else satisfies, Fodor's requirement that a theory of the PAs explain the opacity of PA attributions and the fact that the complements of PA verbs have logical form. The way to put the point is this: Nothing about the ontological account of PAs, or about the character of their supervenience base, explains, or could in principle explain, these features of PA attributions. However, in the manifest image, and hence in the refinement of that portion of its vocabulary (including the PA verbs that will be necessarily found in a psychology of representational phenomena), PAs are attributed by means of *that*-clauses containing embedded content sentences, which are in quasi-quotational contexts. The quotational properties of these contexts explain the opacity of these contexts, and the ambiguity of *that* noted by Cresswell (1985) explains lapses from opacity. Similarly, the fact that it is sentences that stand in these contexts and the fact that sentences have logical form together explain the fact that the contents of PA attributions have logical form, though in a way that says nothing about the nature of the phenomena to which the PA expressions themselves refer, except concerning their semantic properties. In particular, it doesn't entail that PAs themselves have logical form.

The final desideratum on Fodor's list, which, as I noted in chapter 3, is simultaneously the easiest for a theory to satisfy and the hardest, is that any theory of the PAs mesh with the deliverances of empirical psychology. Here I can say only that insofar as there is considerable fertile empirical and theoretical research in cognitive psychology that makes free use of PA locutions and takes seriously the model theory of PA verbs and attributions as relevant to the psychology of human representation (see below), and insofar as none of it, to my knowledge, makes any explicit claims about the supervenience base of the PAs attributed, while identifying the states and processes in question by content, nothing in contemporary psychology is incompatible with the analysis I am offering. And if one examines the programs of such theorists as Johnson-Laird (1983) as well as those of such theorists as Arbib (1987), Marr (1982), and Holland et al. (1987), the explicitly semantic underpinning given to the account of cognitive processes is very much in harmony with the view I am urging. This work, taken together with Cresswell's semantic program, represents a promising development that can only lend empirical support to this naturalistic philosophy of psychology and psychological processes.

It is now time to develop the account of the differences between the intentionality or the representational character of the psychological processes and states of infralingual organisms and machines and that of full-fledged language users, in virtue of which the attribution of PAs to the former is best understood as an attenuated application of predicates that properly apply only in the domain of the psychology of language users.

It is useful to begin this discussion by noting Sellars's crucial distinction that assists is carving off the cognitive abilities of the infralinguistic as of a qualitatively different character from ours and as, in a strong sense, nonconceptual. That distinction is between *sensitivity* and *awareness*. Sellars draws the distinction (using the terms "awareness" and "awareness-*as*") as follows:

> To characterize [a minimal perceptual taking] as a reference *to a red triangle as such* is to classify it as including a sortal which plays the same inferential and non-inferential roles as does 'triangle' in our language, which sortal is modified by an adjective which plays the

same inferential and non-inferential roles as does 'red' in our language.... Thus, to say that an utterance by Jones of a certain term refers *to a red triangle as such* is to classify the utterance in a way which attributes to a knowledgeable user propensities to say such things as:

So, it is not green

So, it has three sides, etc...

Thus, by analogy, the core of the criteria in terms of which we classify a minimal perceptual taking as one of the *of a red trangle as a red triangle* kind is constituted by the inference patterns appropriate to the concepts **red**, **triangle** and, last but not least, **this**. (In general, to specify the 'content' of a conceptual episode is to classify it in terms of the inference patterns appropriate to the concepts involved. (Sellars 1977, paragraphs 85–87)

To be *sensitive* to something (say, a patch of red) is to respond to it in a way distinct from that in which one responds to the rest of the environment. In this sense of "sensitive," thermostats, ammeters, and spectrometers are sensitive to heat, current, and wavelength, respectively. To be *aware* of a patch of red, however, is to be aware of it *as* red—to respond to its redness in the full range (or at least in a wide range) of ways in which it is appropriate to respond to red things: to discuss its color, to compare and contrast its color with other colors, to justify claims about its color by reference to lighting conditions obtaining in observation situations, to infer that it is not blue, and so forth. The most critical requisite is the subject's dispositions to make *inferences* about red things and about redness, for it is in the context of inference and quantification that concepts are most clearly mobilized *as concepts*.

Consider, in this light, what kind of state we ascribe when we attribute a PA to one of our fellows. In chapter 5 I argued that, in the absence of the mastery by the putative believer of the concepts involved in the embedded sentence in a belief ascription, or in the absence of even the most rudimentary knowledge about the subject matter of the embedded sentence, a belief ascription wherein the embedded sentence functions in the quasi-quotational way in which I argue that such sentences must function for the purposes of psychological explanation (that is, as a dot-quoted exemplar of the semantic type of the attributed state) must be false. Another way of putting the point of that argument, in a way that connects directly with the present discussion, is that the possession of the concepts and the basic knowledge relevant to an attributed belief is a necessary condition of having that belief, since without such concepts and knowledge the requisite environment in which the psychological state at issue would function would be so different from that in which the sentence that allegedly characterizes its content is embedded that there would be no sense in which they could be of the same representational type.

Now, we can ask which sort of discriminative ability—sensitivity or awareness—is presupposed in order to have knowledge. Could one be said to know anything about phenomena to which one was sensitive in the primitive sense but of which one was not aware as the kinds of phenomena they are? Clearly the correct answer is "No," for if to know that a patch is red is to mean anything more than to have the kind of competence that a spectrometer has, then to know that it is red is to be aware of it *as* red—to be able to respond to it not only differentially but also appropriately in a wide number of ways. This is what persons who are knowledgeable about colors can do, but something of which spectrometers are entirely incapable. This is why we are knowers and they are mere meters. To be sure, metering is a necessary condition of knowing, but it is far from sufficient.

To have this kind of awareness, and hence to be capable of knowledge, requires that one have a wide range of linguistic, paralinguistic, and conceptual abilities—a sufficiently wide range of abilities to vindicate the claim that one is aware of something as the kind of thing that it is. This is the panoply of abilities that adult humans typically have and that children, dogs, and other infralinguals typically do not. It is this difference in degree of conceptual enrichment that generates a difference in kind of conceptual ability, for it is the difference between an environment wherein a psychological state or event can function semantically in the way that a string of natural language can and an environment that is devoid of the structure of convention and intension that makes such semantic functioning possible. Systems of representational phenomena that meet this condition of inferential and expressive complexity are properly thought of as propositional representational systems.

If animals and other infralinguals are aware only in the more primitive sense of "sensitive", then they have concepts only in a correlatively more primitive sense of "concept", and hence have knowledge in a more primitive and decidedly different sense of "knowledge", and hence even have beliefs in a more primitive sense of "belief". We can characterize this more primitive sense as akin to the states of meters—as *indicating* the state of the internal or external environment, but not as doing so linguistically. Hence, when we attribute such states as PAs to infralinguals, we do not attribute to them states that function in their psychology in the ways in which the embedded content sentences in the ascriptions function in ours. Nothing in their psychological repertoire does. Rather, we ascribe to them representational states that figure in a representational scheme that functions nonconventionally, naturally, as an indicative interface, or as a minimal, impoverished, cognitive map, between the organism and its environment. (See de Vries and Garfield [unpublished] for more on knowledge and conceptual justification.) Any system of phenomena that functions in this indicative fashion counts as a representational system in my sense, but only a subset of these—those with roughly as much logical and conceptual structure as a system of public linguistic representation—counts as propositional.

However, even these nonconventional states and processes cannot be treated individualistically; they must be considered ontologically as broadly supervenient phenomena owing their theoretical allegiance to a psychology that takes seriously the organism in its environmental context. Although the contents ascribed to these representations are not embedded in as rich a system of contents as the one ours are embedded in, and although the factors determining the content of particular infralingual animal or machine representations do not include social linguistic conventions, it is nonetheless surely true that by varying the environment or history of an organism while leaving the internal properties of that organism unchanged we can construct just as compelling a Twin-Earth story about these more primitive representational states as we could construct about their adult human counterparts.

However, to dispel worries about the alleged "infralingual catastrophe," it is not enough to characterize the representational states and processes of infralinguals in a way that does justice both to their representational character and to their nonlinguistic character, though this is half the battle. In order to respond completely to this eliminativist charge, we must also account for the ontogenetic and phylogenetic continuity of psychological complexity between infralingual and language-using organisms.

The problem is posed by the observation that, on the account I have sketched, infralinguals are precluded from being the subjects of PAs in any but a somewhat metaphorical sense. But this would seem to have the consequence that, since our psychological states include PAs and theirs do not, the psychology of the infralinguals should be radically discontinuous with that of language users. It might appear that—surely contrary to fact—this should issue in a complete discontinuity in the principal psychological generalizations satisfied by an organism upon its acquisition of language. Further, since the acquisition of language would seem to require the presence of such things as beliefs regarding the meanings of words, the grammaticality of expressions, and so forth, it would appear that no coherent story could be told about the acquisition process in the absence of a representational system capable of PAs in the language learner. If our story is to be coherent, these problems must be dispelled.

The first problem is solved in part by granting the truth of a portion of the charge while pointing out that the damaging portion is in fact false. There is an important sense in which the psychology of language users is far more complex than that of infralinguals. For one thing, their linguistic competence and performance will figure as explananda in such a psychology, whereas this complex of psychological phenomena will be irrelevant to the psychology of the infralinguals. Moreover, it seems clear from the insinuation of language into the rest of cognitive performance that the complexion of the entire psychological story about an organism will be altered by the presence of language. Thus, there is a perfectly good sense in which psychological discontinuity is not an untoward consequence of this account.

The unsavory aspect of the charge is generated by the suspicion it voices that this discontinuity is so thoroughgoing that the entire mechanism of representation must be different in kind between infralinguals and language users, and hence, presumably, that there can be no interesting sense in which infralinguals can share cognitive properties with language users. A not too hyperbolic way of putting this worry would be to say that this objection envisions the consequence that a prelinguistic child could not share the desire for a drink of milk with his only slightly older but linguistically competent sister. But this worry requires an overstatement of the discontinuity at issue, for the infralingual child or animal is certainly situated in the world and is related to it in countless ways that induce a representational character in its psychological states. What is at issue in distinguishing the character of the infralingual child's or the animal's representational states from ours is not whether they are representational but whether their contents are accurately characterized *propositionally*. And what I have urged is that the repertoire of contents and operations on those contents of which they are capable is insufficient to merit such a rich model. The enrichment of the model comes with the acquisition of the generative, semantic, and logical operations that language makes possible. There is, hence, a perfectly respectable sense in which the toddler can represent milk, and in which the character of this representational state can be such that it guides milk-acquiring behavior, but this does not require the attribution of propositional content to that state, just as the fact that a thermostat turns on a furnace does not require the attribution of a corresponding propositional content to the state of the thermostat although there is a perfectly good (although rather thin) sense in which it represents the temperature.

This observation should also disarm the concern about the possibility of the explanation of language acquisition, for the heart of that concern is the correct observation that it would be difficult to imagine an account of the language-acquisition process that did not advert to processes sufficiently complex internally and in respect of their relations to the linguistic environment to merit characterization as representational. This is the kind of consideration that underlies Fodor's (1975) influential argument for the presence of a full-fledged "language of thought." But, as we have seen, it is fallacious to assimilate *representation* to *having propositional content*, and it would require considerable argument (as well as either artful regress-dodging or dogmatic innatism) to demonstrate that the representational system presupposed at the outset of language learning must be capable of entering into states requiring propositional characterization (though it may well be the case—and I suspect it is—that, as language is acquired at the initial stages, its impact on the general cognitive system is so pervasive that at later stages in the acquisition process propositional representation figures in the story).

These observations should shed more light on the reciprocal primacy of language and representation. I characterized this relation above by saying that whereas nonlinguistic representations are ontologically primitive with respect to public language, public language is epistemologically prior to internal representations. This now emerges as oversimple. It is certainly true that we acquire the vocabulary required for the discussion and conceptualization of representational phenomena *as representational* only through consideration of the semantic properties of public language, and that public language hence serves as our epistemological model and our entré into discourse about our PAs and so eventually into the development of a theoretical vocabulary and a theoretical account of them.

The ontological story is more complex, however. Although animal representation systems are necessary preconditions of the acquisition of language, the possession of PAs is not. To be in a representational state is, from an ontological perspective, to be in a complex set of relations to one's history and environment, and this is so whether the representational state in question is a state of a map, of the ink on this page, of a gerbil, of a computing machine, of an infant, or of an adult human believer. But not all representational states and events inhabit and derive their character from equally rich representational systems. The most complex of these systems require propositional models as their interpretations, and accordingly comprise PAs, among other phenomena, as their members.

But this internal and relational complexity is not achieved by all representational systems. It is true, I have argued, that some set of relations and relata qualifying as a representational system must be present in any object capable of learning language; thus, in this sense, nonlinguistic representation is ontologically (as well as ontogenetically and phylogenetically) prior to linguistic representation. I have also argued, however, that language is a precondition of any animal representation system's acquiring the power that engenders the interpretation of its states and processes as having propositional content. In this sense, language is ontologically prior to the PAs.

With the above sketch of a positive account of the nature of the PAs in hand, we can consider the outlines of a cognitive science of such phenomena as PAs. The three major questions I will address here are the following: Is Stich's charge that the attribution of PAs is so vague and so infected by the point of view of the attributer that the vocabulary of the PAs can play no part in a genuine science accurate? What is the relation between psychology and its neighboring sciences on this account? What can the individualistic study of representational systems contribute to cognitive science?

The only eliminativist charge against the PAs remaining to be answered is Stich's claim that PA attributions are inherently vague and subjective. Recall the reasons for this: First, Stich charges, whereas the criteria of application for any scientific predicate should be relatively determinate, the supposed identity conditions for states and processes individuated by reference to propositional content are in fact similarity conditions, and there are indefinitely many similarity dimensions (e.g., reference similarity, causal-role similarity, ideological similarity) along which PAs get compared. So, whenever we attribute a belief to another, we are really saying nothing more than that their current state is very (but not exactly how) similar on at least one (but possibly more) dimension(s) to a state that, were we in it, we would express using the embedded content sentence in the *that*-clause. This account of PA attribution also lies behind Stich's charge that these attributions are inherently subjective, making essential reference to the states of the PA attributer. These charges are particularly important to consider given the nature of the account I have been urging, for the account of PA attribution I adopt is very similar to Stich's and hence is at least a *prima facie* suspect as viciously vague and subjective in Stich's sense.

One significant difference between my Sellarsian account and Stich's attributer-centered account is this: For Stich, the state to which a subject's state is compared for the purposes of content assignment is that of the attributer. It is this that generates the subjectivity of content assignment, on his account. On my view, however, the reference state for a PA attribution is a token of a public language. It is the objective facts about the meaning in the language of the embedded clause that are relevant for fixing the attributed content, and not the idiosyncratic dispositions or ideology of the attributer.

There are intriguing affinities between this strategy and the Private Language Argument. Any detailed consideration would take us far afield into the contested terrain of Wittgenstein scholarship and exegesis, but note that for Stich the reason that PA attributions are always subjective and indeterminate is that they always involve a direct comparison with the attributer and his or her *own* introspected state. The problem is solved, on the Sellarsian analysis, by taking as the starting point in PA attribution the public role played in a public language by a linguistic token and comparing the state in question with that public object. This introduces a determinacy and an objectivity that necessarily evade the Stichian first-person method. The similarities to Wittgenstein's strategy in demonstrating the primacy of the community and of public practice in determining linguistic and psychological meaning, and to the roles in his account of *use* as the foundation of meaning, are dramatic.

But this straightforward dismissal of the charge of subjectivity leaves the equally serious charge of vagueness untouched. This would appear to be the point at which this account is most vulnerable, for all I have said about what it is to be the subject of a PA is that it is to be (at least in the case of belief) in a relational state that plays the same role in the system of representations that a token of the content sentence that types the state plays in its home language. This is vague stuff. After all, "sameness" here will in general denote, as Stich correctly points out, a relation of similarity rather than one of identity. And the roles that internal tokens play include their connections to sensation and action, which are the kinds of connection that, although they have relevant parallels in relations between public-language tokens, are not to be found literally in the languages in which content sentences are expressed. And, though in virtue of the comparison I urge between public-language tokens and PAs (rather than between the PAs of the attributer and those of the subject) some sources of vagueness are removed, there is still the question of whether we wish to type beliefs according to, say, causal-pattern similarity or reference similarity.

Despite the presence of much vagueness in the conditions of application of a predicate such as "believes that snow is white", I do not believe that these PA predicates are thereby ruled out as useful to psychology. There are two principal reasons for this confidence. In the first place, we have been considering throughout—as is appropriate at this stage of the development of the science and at this stage of the development of this account—the PA predicates as they figure in the language of the manifest image, or at best, in their first refinement as explananda and as explanatory categories in a nascent science of cognition. It is natural for there to be a certain amount of vagueness in predicates figuring at this early stage of the development of a science, which predicates can be expected to be refined in meaning as the science develops.

Second, and more important, however, the kind of vagueness to which I have been alluding may be an ineliminable feature of sciences—I have been arguing that psychology is one—that treat principally of relational properties of their subject matter, which properties may well be irreducible to individualistic properties in virtue of having large, irregular supervenience bases. A pertinent example is the science of ecology. Ecology is replete with properties that are related to individualistic properties of the members of ecosystems in much the same way that I have argued that representational properties are related to the individualistic properties of their bearers, and these properties seem to share the same vagueness. But this does not impugn either their theoretical utility of the credentials of the science.

Consider the property of occupying the canine niche in an ecosystem. This niche is occupied in North America and Asia by such canines as the wolf and coyote. In Africa, it is occupied by the jackal (only distantly related to the other canines) and the hyena (not a canine at all). In Australia, that niche is now occupied by the dingo (a canine, but one imported by *Homo sapiens*), which displaced the native marsupials that once occupied that niche. The maned wolf of the Pampas resembles, both visually and behaviorally, the wolves of North America, but is in fact biologically only distantly related to them. Now, occupying this niche cannot be reduced to any individualistic properties of the occupant. As we have seen, these vary tremendously biologically. It is a matter of certain predatory and scavenging habits, and certain homeostatic roles with respect to ambient prey populations. But the prey, of course, vary depending upon location, climate, and the size of the ·canine·, and the details of the attendant predatory behavior and relations to populations vary accordingly. The respective roles of the maned wolf on the Pampas, the dingo in Australia, and the arctic wolf of the Yukon, are accordingly not exactly the same. They are, rather, similar enough from a theoretical viewpoint to merit their being comprised by the same ecological predicate, which is—despite its vagueness (which issues from the complexity of the relations underlying its instances)—a useful predicate and one that is important to a mature science.

A comparison between "believes that snow is white" in psychology and "occupies the canine niche" in ecology is instructive. The same vagueness that infects the psychological predicate infects its ecological counterpart. In both cases, similarities along a number of dimensions, rather than identity in a single dimension, determine the co-classification of distinct instances. In both cases it is the relations that are borne by the subject in question to a diversity of other individuals that underlie the applicability of the predicate, and in both cases it appears to be the relational and irregular nature of the supervenience base of the predicate that is to blame for this vagueness. But if I am correct about these parallels and about the benign nature of the vagueness of the ecological predicate, then there is no reason to suspect the usefulness to psychology of the PA predicates.

In fact, we can do better than merely suggest the nonuselessness to psychology of the PA predicates. We can demonstrate by means of important examples from exiciting, mainstream research in cognitive science that such naturalistic predicates play an essential role in theories of psychological processes. Consideration of these examples shows that (absent a powerful argument to the effect that the research programs about to be discussed are fundamentally incoherent) the neo-Sellarsian account I have been defending captures current practice far more adequately than either the eliminativist or the reconciliationist views I have rejected. Moreover, I will argue, these examples provide us with a way of understanding not only the role of relational predicates in psychology but also the way they are to be understood in terms of the individualistic predicates, which may explain the capability of organisms to enter into the relations that predicates such as the PAs denote. I will consider first examples from the theory of vision, and then some from recent work on psychological theories and on artificial-intelligence models of induction. Hence, I will examine accounts of infrahumans', humans', and machines' cognitive processes, all of which will turn out to be framed in ineliminably naturalistic terms.

Consider first Arbib's account of visuomotor coordination in toads. Arbib (1987, p. 340) notes that "we have every reason to think of vision as having special circuitry, from the retina of the eye to the tectum of the midbrain and the lateral geniculate nucleus of the thalamus up to a number of regions designated as the visual cortex." One might take this initially as indicating a disposition to treat vision individualistically. But one must be careful to distinguish between an individualistic theory of the wetware or processing underlying an organism's ability to enter into a kind of psychological activity and the account one gives of that process itself, which may advert essentially to more than the underlying neural implementation. In fact, the central construct in the account of early visual processing in humans (Marr and Poggio 1979) and in the explanation of the accuracy of frogs' and toads' prey-acquisition behavior (Ingle et al. 1982; House 1982) is the "depth map" the construction of which is accomplished via vastly different mechanisms by humans and by frogs. This fact itself is significant: The depth map is, on a number of current theories of vision motivated by data from artificial-intelligence models, by psychological data, and by neurophysiological investigation, a central explanatory construct in the psychology of vision. But neither the individualistically characterized neural processes that underlie it nor the computational processes that seem to give rise to it or that manipulate it are constant from species to species. In order to characterize a depth map *as a depth map*, one must characterize it in terms of its relations to the organism's environment and the organism's interaction, visual and motor, with that environment.

More detailed consideration of the models only strengthens this point. Arbib (1987), Arbib and House (1983), and House (1982) present a model of frog depth perception that posits two quite distinct pathways for determining the depth in the visual field of objects such as worms. When locating objects on surfaces, the frog uses an algorithm that relies essentially on contingent geometrical facts about the frog's ecological environment (e.g., that it is made up of relatively continuous surfaces). When locating flying objects, however, the frog relies on focal information from the eyes. In constructing its complete visual map of its environment (necessary for the overall control of complex visuomotor performances), the frog integrates information from both of these sources. Now, the following facts leap out from even this sketchy discussion of Arbib's model: (1) The principal explanatory constructs of the theory are defined and identified relationally—that is, they characterize relations the organism and its internal state bear to its environment. (2) No nonrelational states or characterization of those states could play the same theoretical role they do—internal states with very different individualistic properties are grouped under theoretically important generalizations. (3) The organism's psychological state is characterized by, is explained in terms of, and explains its interactions with, the distal environment. The frog, as a psychological specimen, cannot be understood outside its ecological context; its behavior, and the states and processes causally responsible for it, insofar as they are the objects of useful psychological generalizations, cannot be characterized or explained except in a relational (that is, a naturalistic) vocabulary.

One more philosophically interesting reflection emerges from a consideration of such cognitive neuropsychological studies: The neuroscience (including the computational neuroscience) that explains the capacities, processes, and behavior we have been discussing is, of course, completely individualistic. There is nothing paradoxical about this, but reflecting on this fact does illuminate the germ of truth to be found in both eliminativist and reconciliationist positions: There is an important, individualistic, and nonintentional story that must be told about the frog if we are to complete our understanding of its psychology. That is the story of the neurological processes that *make it possible for the frog to enter into the relations to its environment* which are characterized and explained by the psychology of its visuomotor behavior. But it no more follows from the individualistic, nonintentional character of that story that the psychological story that supervenes in part on it and in part on the behavioral ecology of the frog is individualistic and nonintentional than it would follow from the fact that the explanation of my reproductive fertility is individualistic that my being a parent is an individualistic property of me or is succeptible of an individualistic explanation.

Burge (1987) and Stillings (1987) note that similar morals can be drawn from a consideration of Marr's (1982) theory of human vision. Burge considers four examples of naturalistic features of Marr's account: (1) The explanation of the use by the visual system of zero crossings to detect edges presupposes knowledge of contingent features of the visual environment in which the organism is embedded. Failure to attribute this knowledge *so described* to the system renders this computational process inexplicable; however, describing that knowledge as knowledge, explaining the appropriateness of an organism exploiting it, and explaining its coming to be represented are all naturalistic. (2) The explanation of depth perception via stereopsis similarly involves the exploitation of information about the disparity between images presented by the two retinas. Again, the characterization, account of the use of, and account of the provenance of this information all must proceed naturalistically. (3) and (4) The algorithms that lead to the representations of surfaces *as surfaces* and objects *as objects* are characterized in terms of primitives which are characterized as about kinds of distal objects and about the contingent physical properties and dispositions of those distal objects, and their role in the construction of representations of those objects that are capable of informing thought and action directed toward those objects requires their intentional characterization. Marr's theory of vision—a very powerful and influential theory in artificial intelligence, perceptual psychology, and cognitive neuroscience—presupposes that the organism whose activity it explains is embedded in, and is processing information accurately delivered by, an environment. It characterizes the processes by which that organism comes to represent its environment in terms of their computational and causal relationship to information about distal objects, and it cannot be coherently formulated or understood in nonintentional terms. Again, though the story of the neural implementation of a Marrian perceptual process in an organism may be individualistic, the Marrian theoretical constructs and models, which explain perception *as perception*, are relational and intentional, and capture deep and important generalizations over creatures and machines which may be very dissimilar from any individualistic point of view.

Stillings (1987) further illuminates the naturalistic character of Marrian theories of vision. He notes Fodor's (1980) observation that the working out of a detailed naturalistic program in perception would be parasitic on understanding the physics of the organism-environment interaction, and observes that Marr's account of perception (like Arbib's) characterizes the physics of this interaction, and the organisms' exploitation of the physics of that interaction, in great detail. Stillings points out that the most obvious solipsistic approaches to the theory of vision, involving the use of Fourier transforms to encode the properties of retinal stimulation, have proved hopelessly inadequate as models of the psychology of perception in comparison with the naturalistic Marrian approaches.

It appears, then, that—at least in the case of the psychology of perception, both of infrahumans and of humans—realistic, naturalistic, intentional psychology is alive and well. An eliminativist or a reconciliationist might be expected to retrench at this point, arguing that the fact that the psychology of perception is naturalistic and intentional is not surprising in virtue of the obviously relational character of perception itself. The issue, he or she might be expected to assert, beating a hasty retreat, is whether or not the psychology of central processes—of the PAs themselves—must be characterized relationally (ignoring, of course, the putatively subdoxastic states involved in perception—a move that is itself highly questionable unless one can make good on a very strong modularity thesis regarding visual perception [a thesis cast into grave doubt by Arbib's, Burge's, and Stillings's arguments in Garfield 1987]). In order to lay this final objection to rest, I turn to a brief consideration of the treatment of the psychology of induction offered by Holland, Holyoak, Nisbett, and Thagard (1986). By demonstrating that this powerful theory (endorsed, incidentally, by Dennett and Churchland) employs intentionally construed PA predicates in an apparently realistic context, I complete the empirical demonstration of the superiority of my account over its rivals as a characterization of actual psychological practice.

We can begin, as we did in the case of the psychology of vision, by noting the principal theoretical constructs that inform the model of Holland et al., and then turn to the question of whether these constructs admit of a non-naturalistic treatment. (I take it that the fact that they are of real theoretical utility effectively rebuts—to the degree that consideration of case studies can rebut such claims—any claim to their eliminability, leaving their intentional character as the only bone of contention between my account and those I have criticized.) Holland et al. are frank about what they call the "pragmatic" as opposed to the "syntactic" character of their account:

> Our approach assumes that the central problem of induction is to specify processing constraints that will ensure that the inferences drawn by a cognitive system will tend to be plausible and relevant to the system's goals. Which inductions should be characterized as plausible can be determined only with reference to the current knowledge of the system. Induction is thus highly context dependent, being guided by prior knowledge activated in particular situations that confront the system as it seeks to achieve its goals. *The study of induction, then, is the study of how knowledge is modified through its use.*
>
> Because of its emphasis on the role of the system's goals and the context in which induction takes place, we characterize the theory proposed here as *pragmatic*. In contrast, most treatments of the topic have looked at purely *syntactic* aspects of induction, considering only the formal structure of the knowledge to be expanded and leaving the pragmatic aspects, those concerned with goals and problem-solving contexts, to look out for themselves. In our view, this stance has produced little insight into the way humans do, or efficient machines might, make just the inferences that are most useful. This is not to say that syntactic considerations are irrelevant; indeed, at some level they

are inescapable in any computational system. Our claim is simply that pragmatic considerations are equally inescapable. (1986, p. 5)

The claims made here are highly significant, and are interesting in relation to the morals of the above discussion of vision. Let us pause to note them: (1) Syntactic (that is, solipsistic) accounts of inductive reasoning are taken to be insufficient. (2) The theory of inductive reasoning must be framed in terms of the organism's or machine's knowledge and goals, and of the use to which that knowledge and those goals are put. (3) Although syntactic accounts of processing are relevant to understanding a system's inductive performance, these accounts can provide only a partial explanation of inductive capabilities.

When Holland et al. proceed to specify the knowledge structures to be employed in the explanation of inductive reasoning, this naturalistic, intentional promise pays off. The structures they posit are *mental models* in the sense of Johnson-Laird (1983): models characterized not in terms of the syntax of the neural or computational tokens in which they are implemented but in terms of the representational relations they bear to the world— in terms of their content. The explanatory work they do, which permits generalization over inducing cognitive organisms capable of supporting vastly different representational syntaxes, must (argue Holland et al.) be characterized in terms of what they represent and the properties and relations they ascribe to the objects in the inductive system's cognitive domain. This commitment to characterizing mental models as representational, and hence to characterizing their environment, is explicit: "Because a mental model is the cognitive system's representation of some portion of the environment, and because the relation between the model and the environment is critical to understanding the model's role in the cognitive system, our first step must be a more precise treatment of the environment." (Holland et al. 1986, p. 30)

The theory of Holland et al. is arguably the most comprehensive theory of inductive reasoning on the table. It cannot be dismissed out of hand on *a prioristic* grounds. Its naturalistic, intentional character and its commitment to ascribing knowledge and belief to the creatures in its explanatory domain (prominently including people) certainly count heavily in favor of a theory of psychological practice whereon psychology makes use of intentionally construed, relationally characterized, real, propositional attitudes. (Indeed, it is impossible to imagine a theory of *induction* that does not rely on the reality of belief and the possibility of knowledge, and it would be an odd theory of induction indeed that did not discuss the relations its epistemic subjects bore to their environment.) Thus, *if this theory can be maintained, in anything like its present form, eliminativism and reconciliationism are false.*

Many other examples from contemporary cognitive science could be marshaled as evidence for the empirical claim that, of the accounts of the place of the propositional attitudes in psychology we have considered, only one is really plausible in virtue of accurately characterizing current psychological practice. Eliminativism would force us to reject live, exciting research paradigms as *a priori* bankrupt—a form of philosophical hubris that should be the laughing stock of any practicing cognitive scientist. Reconciliationism requires a solipsism that cognitive scientists studying perception and cognition, those working in neuroscience, artificial intelligence, cognitive psychology, and those working in philosophy (the queen of the cognitive sciences) all find far too restrictive to permit fruitful generalizations over theoretically relevant domains.

At this point we can return at last to the cases of Mary and Mr. Binh. I claimed at the beginning of the book that the account I would advance would resolve the apparent antinomy these cases pose in virtue of the fact that they apparently demonstrate both the necessity and the impossibility of explaining behavior by positing contentful states. We can now see that, despite the difficulties the case of Mr. Binh raises for ascribing such contentful states, we can make good sense of such ascriptions, and that, despite the plausibility the case of Mary assigns to the view that these states are individualistic in character, they need not be.

First, consider Mary. The view I have advanced agrees with Pylyshyn that the psychological state(s) immediately responsible for her exiting the smoke-filled building must "represent the belief that the building is on fire," and that no explanation that adverts only to her individualistically described neural history will explain her exit *under the description* "leaving the burning building"—a description under which we expect to capture the behavior for the purposes of *psychological* explanation. My account diverges from Pylyshyn's however, with respect to what it is to represent the state of affairs *that the building is on fire*. Whereas for Pylyshyn that is an individualistic fact about Mary, for me it is a relational fact; whereas for Pylyshyn some computational state of Mary's central nervous system is to be identified with the belief in question, for me her belief consists in her psychological state's being a ·The building is on fire·, a state with an indefinitely broad supervenience base.

In the case of Binh, where the issues are somewhat more complicated, the story is a bit more complicated as well. Recall Stich's argument that there is simply no fact of the matter as to the content of Binh's belief that Jefferson is a black patriot who made important contributions to logic while building a dry-cleaning empire, in virtue of the following facts: (1) There is no plausible referent for "Jefferson", and hence no reference similarity to any belief we might express with anything like Binh's words. (2) The causal patterns in which that belief is embedded in Binh's psychology are so different from those in which any of our beliefs are embedded, in view of the bizarreness of that belief's history, that there is no sense in which the belief is causal-pattern-similar to any of ours. (3) Since our ideologies in matters pertaining to the "Jeffersons" involved are so widely divergent, there is no belief of ours that would be ideologically similar to Binh's. Hence, Stich concludes, there is no justifiable way to assign content to Binh's state, despite the fact that it is obviously as contentful as any of ours.

Now, the problem with Stich's account of content attribution, as I noted above, is that it makes reference to a relation simply between states of the content attributor and those of the subject of the attributed state. Here the advantage of my account—relying on a quotational device whose interpretation involves a more complex relation between the attributed state, its representational environment, a token of the metalanguage exhibited in the quotational context, and the representational system constituted by that metalanguage—becomes apparent. When we attribute to Binh a relational, broadly supervenient state characterizable as a belief that there is a black patriot and statesman who made significant contributions to logic while building a dry-cleaning empire, we say that he is in a state that is a ·There is a fellow Jefferson, the black patriot and statesman who made significant contributions to logic while building a dry-cleaning empire·. But to attribute this state under this description to Binh is to say that he is in a state that plays the same role in Binh's internal representational system that *that sentence plays in our language*. And, though the dot-quoted sentence surely plays its role very rarely, and though that role is one that it can play only when wielded by a rather deluded speaker of English, it is clear that it does represent a possible state of affairs, one which English is perfectly capable of describing. There is, hence, nothing in principle to prevent us from providing a perfectly determinate (plus or minus the indeterminacy of translation) characterization of even such a bizarre cognitive state as Binh's, even though we ourselves may never be in a state that is in any way similar to his on any dimension of similarity.

Thus, the antinomy presented at the outset of the book has been resolved: It appeared from the tales of Mary and Mr. Binh that we were forced to ascribe individualistic states to persons characterized by content, but that there was in principle no way to individuate states under contentful descriptions. However, by construing such states as relational and by construing content ascription on the dot-quotation model, it is possible to ascribe even the most unusual propositional attitudes to psychological subjects in a perfectly determinate way.

What, then, is the moral of this naturalistic account of representational phenomena for the shape of psychology? Tolman once said:

I would define physiology as a study of the laws determining the *activities* of muscles and glands; I would define psychology as a study of the laws determining the *behavior* of whole organisms; and I would define sociology as the study of the laws determining the *conduct* of groups of organisms.

Accepting these definitions, one's first reaction concerning the interrelations of the three sciences would be to think of physiology as the most basic, psychology as the next most basic, and sociology as the least basic—or, in other words, to conceive of the facts and laws of psychology as dependent upon those of physiology and the facts and laws of sociology as dependent upon those of psychology. But the thesis I am going to try to uphold here is the reverse, and at first sight, seemingly absurd one, to wit: that the facts and laws of psychology are, rather, in some part dependent upon those of sociology and that the facts and laws of physiology are similarly in some part dependent upon those of psychology. (1938, p. 228)

Tolman's argument for this "seemingly absurd thesis" is strikingly similar in many respects to the argument I have been advancing in this book, and strikingly anticipatory of much of the contemporary work to which I have alluded. (Indeed, there is much of Tolman in my account in many respects.) He is concerned with the fact that in order to classify an episode as significant (and hence as psychological) one must pay attention to its social context, and with the fact that in order to classify many physiological events as of the physiological kinds they are (e.g., anxious perspiration) one must know the psychological environment in which they occur.

Now it should be evident that I follow Tolman in taking the inversion of the traditional view of the relation between these sciences seriously. (I also agree with him in resisting a wholesale Hegelian inversion, recognizing that there is also much of foundational interest to a science in all those sciences whose domains comprise the supervenience base of that science. This entails taking both biology and sociology seriously in grounding psychology.) If psychological phenomena such as the propositional attitudes, *qua* psychological, are—considered ontologically—complex semantic, social, and other sorts of relations their bearers stand in to their environment, then it seems indubitable that progress in our understanding of these phenomena will require progress in the relevant social and ecological sciences. In this sense, such sciences as semantics, sociology, perceptual optics, and ecology stand as theoretically fundamental with respect to psychology. This relation is evident in the work of such theoreticians as Arbib, Marr, Holland, Holyoak, Nisbett, Thagard, and Johnson-Laird, all of whom explicitly rely upon these "naturalistic" sciences.

The psychology of infralinguals, of course, will not be so reliant upon the semantic or social ecological sciences, in virtue of their not participating in the social and semantic conventions that engender language and the fully propositional representational systems it makes possible. However, their representational states and processes, as we have seen, nonetheless supervene on, and hence can be fully understood only against the backdrop of, their ecological situation. This point about the foundational nature of the study of the natural and social environment of a representational system in the study of its psychology is nicely anticipated in a very different context by Simon:

> We watch an ant make his laborious way across a wind- and wave-molded beach. He moves ahead, angles to the right to ease his way up a steep dunelet, detours around a pebble, stops for a moment to exchange information with a compatriot.... [His path] is a series of irregular angular segments—not quite a random walk, for it has an underlying sense of direction....
>
> Viewed as a geometric figure, the ant's path is irregular, complex, hard to describe. But its complexity is really a complexity in the surface of the beach, not a complexity in the ant....
>
> *An ant, viewed as a behaving system, is quite simple. The apparent complexity of its behavior over time is largely a reflection of the complexity of the environment in which it finds itself....*
>
> *A man, viewed as a behaving system, is quite simple. The apparent complexity of his behavior over time is largely a reflection of the complexity of the environment in which he finds himself.* (1981, pp. 63–65)

Now, there are to be sure a number of differences in detail between Simon's position and argument and my own, but these need not concern us here. What I want to note here is the recognition by this champion of a computational approach to psychology of the epistemological priority of an understanding of the environment of representational behavior with respect to the characterization of that behavior itself. Seen in this light, the view I am suggesting of the relation between the psychological and the ecological sciences might seem not so radical.

What, then, is the place of individualistic psychology? Is there indeed anything left of it once this naturalistic turn has been made? I have argued that there is an individualistic remainder, and that it has a critical place in the enterprise of cognitive science. The reason for this is that the naturalistic enterprise leaves open the range of questions concerning the mechanisms in virtue of which it is possible for the human (or any other) organism (or machine) to enter into the complex set of relations that issue in its psychological life. After all, not all objects in the natural or the artificial world have psychological lives, and the psychological capacities of objects vary widely. The exploration of the individualistic necessary and sufficient conditions of participating in psychologically characterized activity is hence a critical component of cognitive science. I suspect that many of these questions, once articulated, turn out to have neuroscientific answers (and I take this to be the central kernel of truth in Churchland's account). Again, note the concern of Marr (1982) and Simon (1981) to understand the nature of the individualistic computations underlying the naturalistically characterized phenomena with which they are directly concerned. Accordingly, I would expect, though I cannot present a conclusive argument for this claim, that the bulk of individualistic psychology will be neuroscientific in character. (See Quillen 1986 for an interesting and similar account of the naturalistic character of the PAs and their relation to relevant individualistic states of their subjects.)

There is, however, room for a sort of computational approach to this individualistic enterprise (albeit a fairly restricted form of computationalism), for it may well be—and this is an empirical matter—that the architectures of the organisms and machines that are capable of all or of a certain range of psychological phenomena are naturally characterized in a computational language. Perhaps, as certain functionalists would have it, they are naturally grouped not according to their physical constitutions, which may vary, but according to common computationally characterized properties. This possibility, which certainly emerges in the work of Marr and in that of Holland et al., is, I take it, the kernel of truth in Stich's account.

But it must be remembered that, if this were the case, these individualistic properties, however computationally characterized, would not on that account be *representational*, for all of the many reasons discussed above. The computational predicates they would satisfy would not be their *contents*, but would rather designate noncontentful attributes, which are not of the same descriptive kind as the representational characteristics of the phenomena that might characterize the system at the higher level of descriptions where the PAs emerge. Much of what is individualistic and good in contemporary cognitive science is research that takes this possibility seriously and which is after this computational but not representational characterization of the internal structure of representational systems. The worthy goal of such research is to give us an abstract characterization of the nonrepresentational information processing that underlies the capability of representing organisms and machines to enter into representational activity. But the character of these underlying individualistic phenomena must not be confused with the representational character of the relations they make possible. (Much philosophical commentary on that enterprise has confused it with the study of psychological phenomena *as representational*, either damning it as an inadequate pursuit of that more complex enterprise [Searle 1980] or mistaking progress in such computational research for equal progress on the larger front [Lycan 1981].)

In the course of developing this account, I have been at pains to repeatedly stress the conventionality of my view taken as a whole, despite the perhaps unconventional ontological and methodological theses I have been advancing. In fact, I believe, nothing in my proposals constitutes advice to psychologists or other cognitive scientists to do anything other than what they have been doing. (Perhaps I suggest that one ought to pay more attention to what one's colleagues in semantics, or perception, or neuroscience are up to, but such interconnections are the stuff of good cognitive science anyway.) My argument might also be construed as a gentle nudge in a more naturalistic, sociological direction, but much research is moving in that direction already. The only originality I claim is in correcting the metascientific views that philosophers and philosophically minded cognitive scientists have of the enterprise. Insofar as such correction is needed, it indicates only that the philosophy of cognitive science must pay closer attention to the practice of cognitive science. But that, too, is old advice.

Chapter 8
Summing Up

It is time to draw together all the threads of the argument I have offered, so as to get a synoptic view of the proposal and of its ontological and methodological morals for cognitive science.

In chapter 2 I developed a view of the relation between the scientific enterprise and its ontology, on the one hand, and the manifest image, on the other. Chapter 3 focused specifically on the shape of the corner of the scientific enterprise with which I am concerned—cognitive psychology—and on its ontology and theoretical structure. Several theses important for the subsequent argument emerge from these discussions: The manifest and scientific images make distinct and perhaps competing ontological claims on us. Each presents itself to us as an arbiter of the contents of the world, but the contents presented by the two images are far from identical. In particular, persons and the categories of intentionality, semantic content, and normative evaluation have their origins in the manifest image, and their integration into the image presented by science is problematic. This raises the problem of how to reconcile the competing claims of the images. But even within the scientific image, ontological demands are not made in a single voice. It is often the case that distinct sciences carve reality in different ways. This poses the further problem of how to understand and resolve competing scientific ontologies. While intertheoretic reduction may sometimes vindicate the ontology of a theoretical scheme by locating it within the theoretical ontology of a more secure science, this is not a necessary condition for the realistic interpretation of a science, and it is beside the point for evaluating the claims of the manifest image regarding the reality of its contents. I suggested that the proper way to understand the relation between the images might require taking seriously the claims of both. This discussion left as an open possibility both a multitude of perhaps mutually irreducible facets of the scientific image and the possibility of taking seriously a manifest image that places certain constraints on the conduct of science.

In chapter 3 I was concerned to present an account of the structure of contemporary cognitive psychology. I articulated the model of explanation employed in contemporary cognitive theory (systematic IPS explanation) and the varieties of the dominant account of the ontology of mind (functionalism) embodied by that research program. I argued that the form of functionalism that most accurately characterizes the ontological commitments of current cognitive research is what I called *representational functionalism*—a functionalism that individuates psychological states by reference to their representational character, where this is described in a vocabulary in which such representational predicates as the PA predicates and their cognates appear. I argued that, assuming a realistic view of scientific theories generally, there are no special reasons to adopt an instrumentalist view of theories making use of language ostensibly referring to such phenomena. The central problem for this investigation was hence posed: Given that the PAs as construed by the manifest image must, apparently, be relational in character, relating persons to the contents of their representational events and states, and given the *prima facie* plausibility of the autonomy principle in psychology, it seems that nothing like the PAs, and hence nothing like the phenomena to which representational functionalism appears to be committed, could play a role in a scientific psychology.

Four classes of standard solutions were considered, falling into the four cells determined by two cross-classifications: eliminativist vs. reconciliationist and methodologically individualist vs. methodologically naturalist. I argued in chapters 5 and 6, respectively, that neither the reconciliation of a realistic treatment of the PAs individuated *as* PAs (that is, by reference to their content) with a psychology respecting the autonomy principle nor the elimination of the PAs from the ontology of the manifest image or from that of psychology is possible. The reconciliationist positions, we saw, embodied an unacceptably individualistic theory of the nature of meaningful phenomena. The eliminativists misconstrued the relationship between the manifest image and science and misconstrued the role of human epistemic and doxastic activity in the grounding of the scientific enterprise. Hence, we saw, the only remaining possibility is to recognize the reality of the PAs construed naturalistically and to reject the autonomy principle as a constraint on psychological theory.

The later chapters were devoted to the exploration of the implications of this move. A Sellarsian account of belief and belief attribution was developed which avoided both eliminativist and reconciliationist pitfalls and which met the principal objections to nonindividualistic approaches to psychology and to the rejection of the ontological strictures underlying the autonomy principle.

This view of the nature of the ontology of psychology (more specifically, of the nature of the PAs and other representational phenomena) requires distinguishing mere animal representation systems from their more sophisticated subset, the propositional representation systems of language users, and distinguishing states and processes having computational characterizations from those having representational character. All representational phenomena, including those of infralinguals, are broadly supervenient on nonpsychological phenomena that transcend the boundaries of the organisms or machines that are their subjects. Unlike the PAs, however, which I argued are in a strict sense only states of language users, the representational states and processes of the infralinguals are not supervenient upon such things as social or semantic conventions or on the communities that enforce them, though they do supervene upon their subjects' histories and environment. The irregular nature of these supervenience bases suggests strongly that anything like the reducibility of the ontology or the generalizations of psychology to those of any "more fundamental" physical or individualistic biological science is unlikely, though accommodation in some theoretically relevant sense of psychology to other cognitive and social sciences (or, in the case of infralingual psychology, to the relevant ecological sciences) is more likely. I also argued that the irregularity of this supervenience base and the consequent relative ontological autonomy of psychology with respect to the biological sciences is neither a unique situation among the sciences nor reason to call into question the scientific credentials of psychology. However, I suggested, there is still plenty of room in the enterprise of cognitive science for the individualistic study of the biological and computational underpinnings of the representational *capacities* of organic or mechanical representational systems.

Much of what I have urged must seem odd indeed to anyone steeped in the standard philosophical literature on cognitive science and in the functionalism that pervades contemporary philosophy of mind. It does indeed run against the grain of the methodological vision of the unity of science (which has already fallen out of fashion) and against that of its ontological ghost (which has not been completely exorcised). But it is far from clear that anything I have had to say should appear revolutionary to the practicing cognitive scientist, except insofar as his or her metatheoretic reflections have been influenced by the philosophical orthodoxy. The ontology and the methodology that characterize work within this paradigm are, in virtue of the reliance on the language of representation and in virtue of the growing interpenetration of semantic and psychological research, already characterized by the naturalism I urge.

Some important questions for future philosophical investigation are the following: How are the distinctions between the several propositional attitudes—belief, doubt, hope, fear, desire, etc.—to be drawn? Does belief deserve the primacy it has heretofore been accorded in discussions of the PAs? How are the *prima facie* nonrelational psychological phenomena, such as the qualia, which, like the PAs, appear to straddle the divide between the manifest and scientific images, to be accounted for in psychological theory? What is to be the epistemic and theoretical status of unconscious, perhaps subdoxastic information-processing states which are nonetheless closely theoretically connected to surface representational phenomena? These are but a few of the more specific theoretical questions that I hope will be the subject of further investigation in the near future.

Bibliography

Anderson, J. R. 1976. *Language, Memory, and Thought*. Hillsdale, N.J.: Erlbaum.

Anderson, J. R. 1983. *The Architecture of Cognition*. Cambridge, Mass.: Harvard University Press.

Armstrong, D. M. 1968. *A Materialist Theory of Mind*. London: Routledge and Kegan Paul.

Arbib, M. 1987. "Modularity and Interaction of Brain Regions Underlying Visuomotor Coordination." In Garfield 1987.

Arbib, M., and D. H. House. 1983. "Depth and Detours: Towards Neural Models." In Proceedings of the Second Workshop on Visuomotor Co-Ordination in Frog and Toad: Models and Experiments. Technical Report 83–19, Department of Computer and Information Science, University of Massachusetts, Amherst.

Bach, K. 1982. "*De Re* Belief and Methodological Solipsism." In Woodfield 1982.

Baker, L. R. Forthcoming. "Cognitive Suicide." In Grimm and Merrill (forthcoming).

Baker, L. R. 1987. *Saving Belief: A Philosophical Essay on Mind and Science*. Princeton University Press.

Barwise, J., and J. Perry. 1983. *Situations and Attitudes*. Cambridge, Mass.: MIT Press. A Bradford Book.

Biro, J. I., and R. W. Shahan, eds. 1982. *Mind, Brain, and Function: Essays in the Philosophy of Mind*. Norman: University of Oklahoma Press.

Block, N. 1980a. "Troubles with Functionalism." In Block 1980b.

Block, N., ed. 1980b. *Readings in the Philosophy of Psychology*. Cambridge, Mass.: Harvard University Press.

Block, N., ed. 1981. *Imagery*. Cambridge, Mass.: MIT Press. A Bradford Book.

Burge, T. 1979. "Individualism and the Mental." *Midwest Studies in Philosophy* 4: 73–121.

Burge, T. 1982. "Other Bodies." In Woodfield 1982.

Burge, T. 1987. "Marr's Theory of Vision." In Garfield 1987.

Carnap, R. 1932. "Psychology in Physical Language." *Erkenntnis* 3: 432–465.

Carnap, R. 1947. *Meaning and Necessity*. University of Chicago Press.

Chomsky, N. 1972. *Language and Mind*. New York: Harcourt Brace Jovanovich.

Churchland, P. 1979. *Scientific Realism and the Plasticity of Mind*. Cambridge University Press.

Churchland, P. 1981. "Eliminative Materialism and Propositional Attitudes." *Journal of Philosophy* 78: 67–90.

Churchland, P. 1984. *Matter and Consciousness: A Contemporary Introduction to the Philosophy of Mind*. Cambridge, Mass.: MIT Press. A Bradford Book.

Churchland, P., and P. Churchland. 1982. "Functionalism, Qualia, and Intentionality." In Biro and Shahan 1982.

Cresswell, M. J. 1985. *Structured Meanings: The Semantics of Propositional Attitudes*. Cambridge, Mass.: MIT Press. A Bradford Book.

Cummins, R. 1983. *The Nature of Psychological Explanation*. Cambridge, Mass.: MIT Press. A Bradford Book.

Davidson, D. 1970. "Mental Events." In L. Foster and J. Swanson, eds., *Experience and Theory.* Amherst: University of Massachusetts Press.

Davidson, D. 1977. "The Method of Truth in Metaphysics." *Midwest Studies in Philosophy* 2: 244–254.

Davidson, D. 1984. *Inquiries into Truth and Interpretation.* Oxford: Clarendon.

Davidson, D. 1987. "Knowing One's Own Mind." *Proceedings and Addresses of the American Philosophical Association* 60, no. 3: 441–458.

Dennett, D. 1969. *Content and Consciousness.* New York: Humanities Press.

Dennett, D. 1971. "Intentional Systems." *Journal of Philosophy* 68: 87–106.

Dennett, D. 1975. "Brain Writing and Mind Reading." In K. Gunderson, ed., *Language, Mind, and Knowledge.* Minneapolis: University of Minnesota Press. Also in Dennett 1978a.

Dennett, D. 1978a. *Brainstorms.* Cambridge, Mass.: MIT Press. A Bradford Book.

Dennett, D. 1978b. "Why You Can't Make a Computer That Feels Pain." *Synthese* 38: 415–456. Also in Dennett 1978a.

Dennett, D. 1982. "Beyond Belief." In Woodfield 1982.

de Vries, W. A., and J. Garfield. Concepts, Justification, and Foundations: A Study in Sellarsian Epistemology. Unpublished manuscript.

Fodor, J. 1974. "Special Sciences (or: The Disunity of Science as a Working Hypothesis)." *Synthese* 28: 97–115. Also in Fodor, 1981.

Fodor, J. 1985. *The Language of Thought* Cambridge, Mass.: Harvard University Press.

Fodor, J. 1978. "Propositional Attitudes." *Monist* 61: 501–523.

Fodor, J. 1979. "Three Cheers for Propositional Attitudes." In W. E. Cooper and E. C. T. Walker, eds., *Sentence Processing: Psycholinguistic Studies Presented to Merrill Garrett.* Hillsdale, N.J.: Erlbaum. Also in Fodor 1981.

Fodor, J. 1980. "Methodological Solipsism Considered as a Research Strategy in Cognitive Psychology." *Behavior and Brain Sciences.* 3, no. 1: 63–73. Also in Fodor 1981.

Fodor, J. 1981. *Representations: Philosophical Essays on the Foundations of Cognitive Science.* Cambridge, Mass.: MIT Press. A Bradford Book.

Fodor, J. 1982. "Cognitive Science and the Twin-Earth Problem." *Notre Dame Journal of Formal Logic* 23: 98–118.

Fodor, J., and N. Block. 1972. "What Psychological States Are Not." *Philosophical Review* 81: 159–181. Also in Block 1980.

Garfield, J. 1983. "Propositional Attitudes and the Ontology of the Mental." *Cognition and Brain Theory* 6, no. 3: 319–331.

Garfield, J., ed. 1987. *Modularity in Knowledge Representation and Natural-Language Understanding.* Cambridge, Mass.: MIT Press. A Bradford Book.

Gordon, R. 1986. "Folk Psychology as Simulation." *Mind and Language* 1, no. 2: 158–171.

Grimm, R., and D. Merrill, eds. Forthcoming. *Contents of Thought.* Tucson: University of Arizona Press.

Haugeland, J. 1978. "The Nature and Plausibility of Cognitivism." *Behavioral and Brain Sciences* 1: 215–226. Also in Haugeland 1981a.

Haugeland, J. 1979. "Understanding Natural Language." *Journal of Philosophy* 76: 619–632.

Haugeland, J. 1981a. *Mind Design.* Cambridge, Mass.: MIT Press. A Bradford Book.

Haugeland, J. 1981b. "Semantic Engines: An Introduction to Mind Design." In Haugeland 1981a.

Haugeland, J. 1982a. "Weak Supervenience." *American Philosophical Quarterly* 19: 93–103.

Haugeland, J. 1982b. "Analog and Analog." In Biro and Shahan 1982.

Hellman, G. P., and F. W. Thompson. 1975. "Physicalism: Ontology, Definition and Reduction." *Journal of Philosophy* 72: 551–564.

Hellman, G. P., and F. W. Thompson. 1976. "Physicalism and Materialism." *Nous* 11: 109–145.

Holland, J. H., K. J. Holyoak, R. E. Nisbett, and P. R. Thagard. 1986. *Induction: Processes of Inference, Learning, and Discovery*. Cambridge, Mass.: MIT Press. A Bradford Book.

House, D. H. 1982. "The Frog/Toad Depth Perception System—A Cooperative/Competitive Model." In Proceedings of the Workshop on Visuomotor Co-ordination in Frog and Toad: Models and Experiments, Technical Report 82–16, Department of Computer and Information Science, University of Massachusetts, Amherst.

Ingle, D. J., M. A. Goodale, and R. J. W., Mansfield, eds. 1982. *Analysis of Visual Behavior*. Cambridge, Mass.: MIT Press.

James, W. 1890. *Principles of Psychology*. New York: Dover.

Johnson-Laird, P. N. 1983. *Mental Models*. Cambridge University Press.

Kaplan, D. 1978. "Dthat." In P. Cole, ed., *Pragmatics, Syntax and Semantics*, vol. 9. New York: Academic.

Kim, J. 1978. "Supervenience and Nomological Incommensurables." *American Philosophical Quarterly* 15: 149–156.

Kim, J. 1982. "Psychophysical Supervenience." *Philosophical Studies* 41: 51–70.

Kim, J. 1984a. "Epiphenomenal and Supervenient Causation." *Midwest Studies in Philosophy* 9: 257–269.

Kim, J. 1984b. "Concepts of Supervenience." *Philosophy and Phenomenological Research* 45: 153–176.

Kitcher, P. 1984. "In Defense of Intentional Psychology." *Journal of Philosophy* 81: 89–106.

Kiteley, M. 1968. "Of What We Think." *American Philosophical Quarterly* 5: 31–42.

Kiteley, M. 1985. Subjectivity's Bailiwick and the Person of its Bailiff. Unpublished manuscript.

Lewis, D. K. 1975. "Psychophysical and Theoretical Identification." *Australasian Journal of Philosophy* 27: 291–315.

Lewis, D. K. 1979. "Attitudes *De Dicto* and *De Se*." *Philosophical Review* 88: 513–543.

Lewis, D. K. 1980. "Mad Pain, Martian Pain." In *Readings in the Philosophy of Psychology*, Vol. 1, ed. N. Block. Cambridge, Mass.: Harvard University Press.

Loar, B. 1981. *Mind and Meaning*. Cambridge University Press.

Lycan, W. 1981. "Toward a Homuncular Theory of Believing." *Cognition and Brain Theory* 4: 139–160.

Lycan, W. 1983. "Form, Function, and Feel." *Journal of Philosophy* 78: 24–49.

Lycan, W. Thoughts About Things. Unpublished manuscript.

Marr, D. 1982. *Vision: A Computational Investigation in the Human Representation of Visual Information*. San Francisco: Freeman.

Marr, D., and T. Poggio. 1979. "A Computational Theory of Human Stereo Vision." *Proceedings of the Royal Society of London* B204: 301–328.

Marras, A., ed. 1972. *Intentionality, Mind, and Language*. Champaign: University of Illinois Press.

McGinn, C. 1982. "The Structure of Content." In Woodfield 1982.

Montague, R. 1963. "Syntactical Treatments of Modality, with Corollaries on Reflexion Principles and Finite Axiomatizability." *Acta Philosophica Fennica* 16: 153–166.

Montague, R. 1979. "The Proper Treatment of Quantification in Ordinary English." In J. Hintikka, J. Moravcsik, and P. Suppes, eds., *Approaches to Natural Language*. Dordrecht: Reidel.

Newell, A., and H. Simon. 1976. "Computer Science as Empirical Inquiry: Symbols and Search." *Communications of the Association for Computing Machinery* 19: 113–126. Also in Haugeland 1981a.

Perry, J. 1979. "The Problem of the Essential Indexical." *Nous* 13: 3–21.

Putnam, H. 1960. "Minds and Machines." In A. Anderson, ed., *Minds and Machines*. Englewood Cliffs, N.J.: Prentice-Hall.

Putnam, H. 1975a. "The Meaning of 'Meaning'." In K. Gunderson, ed., *Language, Mind, and Knowledge*. Minneapolis: University of Minnesota Press. Also in Putnam 1975b.

Putnam, H. 1975b. *Mind Language, and Reality: Philosophical Papers, Volume 2*. Cambridge University Press.

Putnam, H. 1981. *Reason, Truth, and History*. Cambridge University Press.

Pylyshyn, Z. 1980. "Cognition and Computation: Issues in the Foundations of Cognitive Science." *Behavioral and Brain Sciences* 3: 111–132.

Pylyshyn, Z. 1984. *Computation and Cognition: Toward a Foundation for Cognitive Science*. Cambridge, Mass.: MIT Press. A Bradford Book.

Quillen, K. 1986. "Propositional Attitudes and Psychological Explanation." *Mind and Language* 1, no. 2: 133–157.

Quine, W. V. O. 1960. *Word and Object*. Cambridge, Mass.: MIT Press.

Searle, J. 1980. "Minds, Brains, and Programs." *Behavioral and Brain Sciences* 3: 417–457.

Searle, J. 1983. *Intentionality: An Essay in the Philosophy of Mind*. Cambridge University Press.

Sellars, W. 1956. "Empiricism and the Philosophy of Mind." In H. Feigel and M. Scriven, eds., *Foundations of Science and the Concepts of Psychology and Psychoanalysis*. Minneapolis: University of Minnesota Press. Also in Sellars 1963.

Sellars, W. 1960. "Philosophy and the Scientific Image of Man." In R. Colodny, ed., *Frontiers of Science and Philosophy*. University of Pittsburgh Press. Also in Sellars 1963.

Sellars, W. 1963. *Science, Perception, and Reality*. London: Routledge and Kegan Paul.

Sellars, W. 1974. "Meaning as Functional Classification." *Synthese* 27: 417–437.

Sellars, W. 1977. "Descartes and Berkeley: Reflections on the New Way of Ideas." In P. Machamer and R. Turnbull, eds., *Studies in Perception: Interrelations in the History and Philosophy of Science*. Columbus: Ohio State University Press.

Sellars, W. 1980. "Behaviorism, Language, and Meaning." *Pacific Philosophical Quarterly* 61, no. 1–2: 3–25.

Sellars, W. 1981. "Mental Events." *Philosophical Studies* 39: 325–345.

Simon, H. 1981. *The Sciences of the Artificial*. Cambridge, Mass.: MIT Press.

Sellars, W., and R. Chisholm. 1972. "Correspondence on Intentionality." In Marras 1972.

Smart, J. J. C. 1959. "Sensations and Brain Processes." *Philosophical Review* 68: 141–156.

Stalnaker, R. Semantics for Belief. Unpublished manuscript.

Stich, S. 1983. *From Folk Psychology to Cognitive Science: The Case Against Belief*. Cambridge, Mass.: MIT Press. A Bradford Book.

Stillings, N. 1987. "Naturalism in Theories of Vision." In Garfield 1987.

Stillings, N., M. Feinstein, J. Garfield, E. Rissland, D. Rosenbaum, S. Weisler, and L. Baker-Ward. 1987. *Cognitive Science: An Introduction*. Cambridge, Mass.: MIT Press. A Bradford Book.

Thomason, R. H. 1977. "Indirect Discourse is Not Quotational." *Monist* 60: 340–354.

Tolman, E. C. 1922. "A New Formula for Behaviorism." *Psychological Review* 29: 140–145. Also in Tolman 1951.

Tolman, E. C. 1936. "Operational Behaviorism and Current Trends in Psychology." In *Proceedings of the 25th Anniversary of the Inauguration of Graduate Studies, University of Southern California*. Also in Tolman 1951.

Tolman, E. C. 1938. "Physiology, Psychology, and Sociology." *Psychological Review* 45: 228–241. Also in Tolman 1951.

Tolman, E. C. 1948. "Cognitive Maps in Rats and Men." *Psychological Review* 55: 189–208. Also in Tolman 1951.

Tolman, E. C. 1951. *Behavior and Psychological Man*. Berkeley: University of California Press.

Tuomela, R. 1985. *Science, Action, and Reality*. Dordrecht: Reidel.

Van Fraassen, B. 1980. *The Scientific Image*. Oxford: Clarendon.

Wartenburg, T., and D. Ross. 1983. "Quine and the Third Manual." *Metaphilosophy* 14: 267–275.

Woodfield, A. 1982. *Thought and Object: Essays on Intentionality*. Oxford: Clarendon.

Index